Goal Setting

What You Need to Know About Setting Goals and How to Create Action Plans and Habits for Success that Don't Require Immense Willpower

Contents

Introduction

Do you think you get everything you want in life? Have you set goals for yourself in the past and accomplished them? Do you even know what your goals are? Don't worry if your answer is no to all these questions. You aren't alone if you are struggling with this. However, if you wish to succeed, then you must spend some time thinking about all the things you want in life.

Who doesn't want to succeed in life? Sadly, not many people know where or how to start. What differentiates the massive chunk of the general population from all those who succeed? No, it is not wealth, success, popularity, or sheer luck. The only factor that differentiates successful people from the rest is their power of choice. They consciously turned their lives around and create the future they wanted. To do this, they set goals for themselves. They not only set goals, but they ensured that they gave it their all to attain those goals.

If you put your mind to it, there is nothing you cannot achieve. All you need to do is realize what you want to achieve and then give it your all. Think of it as a slight push in the right direction. Add in some effort, and you accomplish your goals. Well, this is precisely what this book does for you.

When you set certain goals in life, you will have a sense of direction. Without a goal, you get nowhere, and procrastination will inevitably set in. A goal brings clarity and vision in life. When these things are present, you will automatically do everything to turn your goal into a reality. There are different aspects of your life you can set goals in, ranging from your personal to professional life. Setting and attaining goals need not be a complicated process. It all starts with understanding who you are and what you want in life. Once you identify your core values and beliefs, it becomes easier to understand who you are. When you know who you are, it becomes easier to develop goals in sync with your core values. Don't worry if all this seems a little scary right now. After you go through the information in this book, setting and attaining goals will seem quite doable.

In this book, you will learn about the meaning of setting goals, the benefits it offers, personality traits and goals, the pitfalls of SMART goals, and how to attain your goals. You will also learn to identify your mission, vision, and core values, while furthering the understanding of your goals using "WHY" and "HOW" you want to attain them. Besides all this, you will learn about simple hacks for lazy goal setting, mind mapping, the power of vision boards, time management, and tips to attain your goals. When you learn to identify obstacles or mistakes in goal setting, it becomes easier to take corrective action. This book also provides information about the importance of focus, motivation, and self-discipline. This book is your one-stop guide to setting and attaining goals.

By creating actionable plans and learning good habits, you can attain your goals, even if you lack willpower and motivation. To be successful, all that you need to do is follow the information in this book. So, if you are ready to learn more about all this, then let us get started without further ado.

Chapter One: So Why Set Goals?

What are Goals?

Take a moment and try to answer this question, "What do you want in life?" Think about all the things you wish to attain. It's quite likely that you will be able to list various things like leading a happy and successful life, carving a successful career, maintaining good relationships, improving your bank balance, and so on. Usually, most of us have brilliant ideas, but these ideas are never materialized. At the smallest sign of inconvenience, an inexperienced risk-taker convinces himself that it is the end of the world, and he will retreat.

Once you pursue your goals, you will be in a place where taking sensible risks becomes easier. Unless you take risks, you accomplish nothing in life. When you take a risk, you must prepare yourself to be criticized and even prepare yourself to second-guess whatever decision you make. While understanding any resistance to the goals you have set, think about the different things that can go wrong and be flexible enough to overcome any objections to your adopted approach. Who doesn't want to succeed? However, there are two essential qualities many people lack, and these are patience and persistence. It is where goals come into the picture.

A goal is a specific and quantifiable objective you wish to attain within a given timeframe. There is a direct and strong correlation between the effort you make to achieve them and realizing the goal with goals. Unlike a dream or a wish, mostly based on wishful thinking and sheer luck, goals can be easily divided into short-term objectives that become checkpoints to ensure you are on the right track. Therefore, a goal is the aim of specific action to attain a predefined standard of proficiency within a specific timeframe. It helps you understand the level of competence you wish to attain while creating useful parameters to measure your current performance.

What is Goal Setting?

Goal setting is a conscious process you undertake to attain goals. The importance of setting a goal and the entire process of setting goals must never be overlooked. The way your life turns out depends on how you choose goals and the way you perceive them. If you go about life with a passive attitude, you cannot accomplish anything. The goal-setting theory is based on a simple idea that conscious goals determine your action and that your individual goals influence conscious human behavior. To simplify it, goal setting helps you decide what is good for your welfare and then prompts you to realize those goals through conscious action.

Whenever you ask the question, "What is goal setting?" remember that goals differ from one person to another. A variety of factors ranging from lifestyle to values and your definition of success define your goals. Therefore, your goals will be unique to you, and don't be bothered if they are not like someone else's goals. The classic definition of goal setting essentially comes down to a simple process of identifying something you wish to attain and then defining various measurable objectives and a timeframe to achieve that objective. There are different areas where you can set goals. You can set financial goals, lifestyle goals, health goals, fitness goals, and so on.

Learning to set goals in different areas of your life makes it easier to accomplish your desired outcome.

Principles of Setting Goals

There are certain principles upon which goals are based. In this section, let us look at the different principles of goal setting.

Commitment

Your attachment to the goal and the degree of determination to attain it, despite facing obstacles, is known as commitment. The chances of attaining your goals significantly increase when you are committed to them. If you discover that your performance level is less than optimum, then commitment to the goal ensures that you have the inherent motivation to adjust your performance to attain the goal. When you are not committed, especially when it comes to challenging goals, the chances of giving up on the goal increase. After all, we are more inclined toward doing things we intend to accomplish. Various factors influence one's commitment levels. The desirability of a goal and the ability to attain it are the primary factors influencing your commitment level. If you want to be successful, you must possess an inherent desire and a thorough understanding of all required for attaining your goals.

Clarity

The goals you set for yourself must be clear. If the goal is vague, then the motivational value associated with it is relatively low. Setting clear, unambiguous, and precise goals ensures you can measure your progress. When the goal is clear, you better understand all the tasks you must accomplish to attain the goals.

Challenge

Regardless of the goal you set for yourself, ensure that it is attainable but is also challenging. Your performance improves when you tackle a challenging goal. It, in turn, improves your levels of self-satisfaction and motivation to find suitable strategies to unlock your potential. If the goal you set is unattainable, it will merely make you feel unsatisfied and even frustrated.

Complexity

Task complexity is another principle you must adhere to while setting goals. If the goal is complicated or out of your skillset's purview, it can become overwhelming. It can harm your productivity, morale, and motivation to attain the goal. The time limit you set to attain a goal must be realistic. Giving yourself sufficient time to attain a goal provides opportunities for reassessing the goal's complexity while enabling you to improve your performance. Even if you are motivated, you can become overwhelmed if the goal is complicated for your existing skillset.

Feedback

Feedback, whether or not it is internal or external, helps determine your progress and how much the goal has been accomplished. An unambiguous system of feedback ensures the desired action is taken whenever necessary. If your performance is below the required performance needed to attain a goal, feedback gives you a chance to reflect upon the progress you make. When you do this, it becomes easier to take corrective action.

Benefits of Setting Goals

The first step toward turning any of your dreams into reality is through establishing specific goals. In this section, let us look at some of the benefits you can reap by setting goals for yourself.

Measuring Your Progress

You can track no progress you make unless you have a specific goal in mind. Tracking and measuring the progress you make is gratifying and self-satisfactory. Whenever you see you are moving in the right direction and are a step closer to attaining your goal, it gives you the motivation required to keep going. It helps you stay focused, keep a level head, and feel energized. For instance, let us assume that your goal is to run 10 miles. If you aren't aware of your starting point or the destination you want to reach, it becomes difficult to track how long these 10 miles will be. If you aren't aware of the time taken to reach the destination, tracking any progress you make becomes exceedingly difficult. In the same situation, if you had a specific route and time frame in mind, then you can easily track and measure the progress you make. Every mile you run brings you a step closer to attaining your goals. Goals also ensure that your motivation levels stay high. At times, it becomes easy to feel discouraged when you haven't attained a goal. In such situations, if you can see all the progress you made, you will instantly feel better about yourself.

Provides Focus

Without a specific goal in mind, any effort you make will feel disjointed and confusing. If you are unsure of what you are trying to achieve, it can cause wasted time and effort. Time and effort are two precious resources you cannot afford to squander in life. Have you ever seen a hummingbird take flight? It often looks erratic, unfocused, and confusing. Without a goal, this is pretty much how you go about your life. Now, have you seen a hawk swoop down and catch its prey? When you have a goal, your focus becomes concentrated, and you can divert all your resources toward attaining your goals. After all, all the resources are finite, and their uses are infinite. A goal helps prioritize and then shift all your focus toward attaining them. It enables you to make the most of all the resources and opportunities available to you.

Motivation Levels

When you have no goals in mind, it is easy to put off work until a later date. For instance, if an athlete knows he needs to get in shape for a specific event, he will work out every day. Whether or not he feels good about it or not, he must keep working out and exercising to ensure that he attains his goals. He will keep working toward his goals even when he feels tired or sore. He will do this because he knows he needs to get in shape for a specific event. If he had no idea of an exact destination in his mind, then what would motivate him to keep working out? Why would he want to work out when he doesn't feel like it? To avoid all this, it is quintessential that you set specific goals for yourself.

Improve Productivity

Whenever you attain a goal or accomplish it, it makes you feel successful. Once you get the taste of success, you will want to keep experiencing it repeatedly. It gives you the motivation to push yourself harder and toward the next rung of the success ladder. It enables you to challenge yourself to shatter the glass ceiling and try to accomplish even more. When you work toward attaining and surpassing the goals you set for yourself, you can achieve more than you ever thought was possible.

Overcome Procrastination

Procrastination is something we all tend to indulge in occasionally. Regardless of how motivated you are toward attaining the goal, procrastination creeps in. Whenever you set a goal, you must always establish a timeframe for attaining that goal. When there is a timeframe to work within, it helps reduce the chances of procrastination. If you know you must complete five tasks within 24 hours, you can practically avoid procrastinating because you have to complete those goals. If there is no time limit to attain a goal, then it is likely that you will keep telling yourself, "I will do it later," or "I will do that tomorrow." Once procrastination gets hold of you, it becomes exceedingly difficult to take any positive action.

By setting goals, you will finally understand how dangerous procrastination can be. Whenever you waste time, it means you have wasted another hour or another day and are moving away from your goals. It enables you to rethink your stance toward attaining your goals. Also, it helps prioritize all the tasks you must accomplish to achieve the goals you have set.

Contemplation

By setting goals, you are forced to understand what you wish to attain in life. Goals help you understand what you want from yourself and life in general. A couple of simple questions you might have to answer while doing this are as follows.

- What is your desired level of income?
- What is your ideal level of success?
- What do you want your life to look like?
- What kind of financial support should you attain your goals?
- What are your dreams and aspirations?

Once you have answered these questions, you will have a specific result in mind. This result can be easily broken down into measurable and attainable goals.

All these goals ensure that you stay motivated, overcome procrastination, and concentrate on attaining your dreams. To live your best life possible, then you must set, achieve, and surpass your goals.

Chapter Two: Goals and Your Personality Type

Goal Setting and Personalities

Before you set any goals for yourself, it is crucial to determine your personality type. Goal setting is a journey that begins with you. Therefore, it is quintessential you know all the things that make you unique, how you work, and things that make you tick. Your behaviors, interests, and motivations are some factors that determine the goals you set. Since all these factors are the byproducts of your personality, you must understand yourself before setting any goals.

Everyone is unique, so you're the only one who can understand what makes you tick. By profiling, it gives you a better insight into yourself. Take a moment and think about some successful people. How do these people usually act or behave? What are their basic traits? Do you think these traits helped them succeed? If yes, then how do you fare when you compare yourself to these people? Do you think some of your characteristics or traits are preventing you from succeeding?

Some traits are conducive to success and achievement. However, even if you don't possess them, it doesn't mean you are doomed to fail. It just means you must learn of the different characteristics that enable you to meet your goals and use them to your advantage. We all have certain characteristics that hold us back. So, it is time to turn negative traits into positive ones that can lead you toward success.

Behavioral preferences, intelligence preferences, and personal motivation are the primary personal indicators that influence what you do, how you relate to others, your chances of success, and your thinking process. We all behave differently toward different things. This natural behavior is unique to all individuals, and it influences the way you view success and failure. Your behavioral preferences essentially influence your general attitude in life. By understanding your natural behavior tendencies, you'll have a better idea of how this impacts the goals you set and your chances of attaining them. Intelligence preferences mean we are all good at various things, and it influences the goals we set for ourselves. By understanding your interests, you can determine your natural aptitude. No, this differs from an IQ test. Instead, you are merely trying to determine your primary aptitude. If the goal you set is not in sync with your natural aptitude, it becomes challenging to work toward achieving it. We all have different factors that motivate us. Some of these factors are inherent to our personality, while others are based on life situations. Understanding your personal motivations is quintessential to determine whether you can attain a goal or not.

Now, it is time to understand who you are as an individual and its implications. For setting your goals and working toward becoming successful, there are various self-assessment tests available online. It hardly takes a couple of minutes to complete one of these tests. The most popular personality indicator test is the Myers Briggs Personality test.

Determining the Personality Type

According to the Myers Briggs personality test, every personality type can be described using four-letter codes, such as INFP, ESTJ, ESFP, etc. Each specific letter signifies a critical aspect of the individual's overall personality. This theory suggests that even seemingly random variations in an individual's behavior are usually predictable. These variations occur due to specific differences in how individuals approach different functions like thoughts, interaction, and behavior. All these individual differences can be combined by using the Myers Briggs personality dichotomies. Each class of dichotomies consists of different and opposing styles of personality, like introversion versus extraversion. Let us understand more about the four dichotomies.

● Sensing (S) vs. Intuition (N) - This dichotomy describes how an individual absorbs information.

● Extraversion (E) vs. Introversion (I) - This dichotomy describes how individuals obtain their personal energy.

● Thinking (T) vs. Feeling (F) - This dichotomy describes how individuals tend to make decisions.

● Judging (J) vs. Perceiving (P) - This dichotomy describes how an individual tends to organize his world.

Extraversion

Extroverts are energized whenever they spend time around others and in public settings. Such people love being the center of attention and thrive on the energy of those around them. Extroverts love to speak their minds, and they are not reserved. They are usually popular and well-liked by others. If an extrovert doesn't spend sufficient time with others, he can feel drained. They love participating in group activities and attending parties. They are enthusiastic, animated, and are termed as gregarious. An extrovert's communication style is verbal and assertive. They think more straightforwardly when expressing themselves, and they love staying in the limelight. The primary characteristics of this personality include assertiveness, talkativeness, enthusiasm, and outgoing nature.

- Do you love attending parties and working in groups?

- Do you feel invigorated whenever you interact with others?

- Do you love engaging in conversations with anyone and everyone?

- Do you have plenty of friends?

- Do you think you are easily approachable?

- Do you love sharing information about yourself?

- Do you like meeting new people?

Introversion

Individuals who lean toward introversion are often characterized by their desire to concentrate on the world within them instead of the external world. They love spending time by themselves or with a select group of individuals. They feel drained whenever they spend prolonged time in public or large groups. Deep relationships matter more than inconsequential small talk. They value quality over quantity with their friend circle. They are good at listening and always think before talking. Before they express themselves, they often spend some time and process all the information internally. The primary characteristics of this personality trait include an increased need for privacy, deliberation, and independence.

- Do you feel better when you spend time with yourself?

- Do you love spending time by yourself?

- Do you feel drained whenever you spend prolonged periods in public settings?

- Do you like keeping to yourself?

- Do you have a small friend circle?

- Do others describe you as a good listener?

Sensing

Individuals with a dominant sensing personality often stay focused in the moment. They are the individuals who love living in the moment and can be described as "here and now" people. They are highly factual and process all the information using their five senses. They are literal and concrete thinkers, enabling them to see things the way they are, instead of how they wish they should be. They like trusting only those things that are certain. Realism and commonsense are two values that sensors cannot do away with. They love indulging in ideas with practical applications. The primary characteristics of this personality trait include the ability to stay realistic, factual, and practical.

- Do you live in the moment?
- Are you always aware of your surroundings?
- Do you notice small details that others often miss?
- Do you allow your senses to guide your decision-making?
- Do others describe you as being practical?

Intuition

These individuals live in the future and are always thinking about various possibilities the world offers. All the information they process is based on impressions and patterns they notice in the information. Inspiration and imagination are significant to intuitive people. They love gathering knowledge and often read between the lines. Their inherently abstract nature enables them to see the big picture and attracts them to profound ideas or concepts. The essential traits of this personality include inventiveness, imagination, abstract thinking, and idealism.

- Do you often spend a lot of time thinking about what the future holds in store for you?
- Do you like daydreaming about how your future would be?
- Are your ideas more theoretical than practical?

- Do you see things how you wish they were supposed to be instead of how they truly are?

Thinking

These people are incredibly objective, and all their decision-making is based on facts and figures. They depend on reliable information they can see and process. Their heads guide them instead of their hearts. They judge situations and the world around them based on their logic. They always value the truth over tact and can quickly notice any flaws that others don't. They are critical thinkers who love taking an objective approach toward solving a problem. However, it doesn't mean these people are devoid of emotions. The basic characteristics of this trait include the ability to stay logical, objective, rational, critical, and impersonal.

- Do you always decide with your head?

- Do you always seek the truth, regardless of its consequences?

- Do others describe you as thick-skinned?

- Are you firm with people?

Feeling

Unlike the thinking personality, these people are subjective. Most of their decision-making is based on values and principles. They use their hearts instead of their heads for making decisions. They judge situations, others, and the world based on the circumstances and their feelings. They like being appreciated and always aim to please others. Harmony and empathy are more important than any other trait for these individuals. This trait's basic characteristics include the ability to be gentle, warm, empathetic, and passionate.

- Do you hate conflict?

- Do you always decide with your heart?

- Do your emotions drive all your decisions?

- Do you consider what others might feel because of your decisions?

- Do you get hurt rather easily?

Judging

These individuals love order and organization in all aspects of their lives. They are often termed *sequential thinkers*. They love living their lives according to schedules and structures. They enjoy seeking closure and completing all the tasks they start. They love working with deadlines and take them seriously. Unless they complete their work, they cannot indulge in anything else. The judging preference doesn't mean they are judgmental. It merely refers to how an individual deals with his daily activities. The basic characteristics of this personality include control, organization, structure, and decisiveness.

- Are you good at completing all the tasks you start?

- Do you like staying organized and like sticking to schedules?

- Do you often complete tasks quickly?

- Do you complete one plan and only then move onto the next plan?

- Do you like ensuring that all the tasks you start will reach a logical conclusion?

Perceiving

The perceiving preference makes an individual flexible and adaptable. They love keeping their options open and are random thinkers. They thrive when there is no fixed schedule and love the unexpected. They usually multitask and are spontaneous. They love starting tasks more than completing them. Deadlines are usually suggestions for them, and they indulge in plenty of procrastination. They love to play while they work. This personality's basic characteristics include adaptability, spontaneity, flexibility, and a relaxed attitude toward life.

- Are you carefree and spontaneous?

- Do you hate routines and schedules?

- Do you usually procrastinate?

- Do you often have a change of heart while completing tasks?

- Do you flit from one task to another?

- Do you like keeping your options open?

Setting Goals Based on Personality Types

There are four dichotomies, and by using permutations and combinations, you will end up with 16 primary types of personalities. Each personality is a 4-letter abbreviation of the primary traits discussed above. For instance, ESFP personality traits refer to an individual who leans toward extraversion, sensing, feeling, and perception instead of introversion, intuition, thinking, and judging. Likewise, an individual with an INTJ personality leans toward introversion, intuition, thinking, and judging. All the personality dichotomies are present in every individual. However, one trait is usually more dominant than the other, and this is how personalities differ.

ENTJ

Individuals with this personality trait are often ambitious, dream big, and feel happy whenever they take any action for attaining their goals. While setting goals, ensure that you allow yourself to dream big and keep planning. Even if your goal seems complex and challenging, your driven mind and basic personality traits will ensure that you keep going.

INTJ

This personality type is fond of setting goals: a logical, well-defined, and organized future appeals to the rational mind of the INTJ personality. Your logical mind will enable you to set goals and develop a plan of action to attain those goals. Besides that, you can also easily think about all the obstacles you might face to avoid the same in the future.

ENFJ

This personality type is focused. They love spending most of their time ensuring those around them are happy in the present and the future. While setting goals, don't overlook this inherent tendency you might have. Try to choose those goals that not only improve the quality of your life but help others too. If this doesn't seem possible, try choosing those goals that will not harm others. If there is any conflict of interest, your motivation to keep going might disappear, and you will feel disappointed.

INFJ

This personality type is usually averse to setting goals. They are spontaneous and are driven by their feelings. Since the feelings of right and wrong drive them, their goals can change from one moment to another. So, while setting goals, ensure that your mind and heart are in sync with the goal you have chosen. Regardless of the area of your life you are working on, ensure that your mind and heart are in complete and total alignment. If there is any conflict of interest between these two, your chances of succeeding will reduce.

ENFP

This personality type is open to exploring the world and loves new things. However, it can be slightly problematic while setting and achieving goals. They can set goals easily but usually get bored and abandon them for anything better that comes along. Therefore, ensure that you establish a couple of measures of how to stay on track. Also, your goals must completely align with your core values and beliefs.

INFP

This personality type finds setting and working toward goals rather constraining. They love change, act according to their internal desires, and don't like being tied down to a specific thing. This can become problematic while setting goals. Therefore, try to concentrate on the bigger picture whenever you set goals. By concentrating on this, you will have the desire to keep going. Also, the bigger picture must be in sync with your deepest desires.

ENTP

This personality type loves to dream big. However, the only problem is that they often have trouble staying on the right track. They love to explore, and sticking to one goal for too long doesn't appeal to them. If you are this personality type, ensure that you keep feeding your brain various distractions to ensure that you stay on the right track. If you keep thinking about one goal, you will easily get bored. So, ensure that you concentrate on all the aspects of your life while working toward the goal.

INTP

The idea or the art of setting goals doesn't come naturally to this personality type. They are dreamers and rarely have a concrete idea of the future they desire. So, setting goals can become a little tricky. However, if you develop a structured approach to attaining your goals, you can easily circumvent this problem. Ensure that the goal you are working toward is something you honestly desire and want in life. If you do this, the chances of your mind wandering while working toward a goal will reduce. You can also set up a support system to ensure that you are on the right track.

ESTJ

This personality type loves setting goals and loves the idea of successfully completing all the tasks they put their minds to. As long as your goals are practical, the chances of attaining them are high. This personality type also loves to live in the present and do things immediately.

ISTJ

Patience and determination are two key traits of this personality type. Integrity and following through is critical to this personality type. They also like working quietly and without creating a fuss about all that they have to achieve. They derive pleasure when they strike things off their to-do list.

ESFJ

This personality type loves getting things accomplished and are often task-oriented. It makes them happy to set goals and work toward attaining those goals. However, the only problem you must know is this personality type focuses a little too much on the present. So, to be successful, and attain your goals, ensure that you consider the bigger picture. Think long-term and not just the short-term while setting goals.

ISFJ

Reliability, hard-working nature, and patience are the primary characteristics of this personality type. Therefore, working toward and attaining goals is something they love doing. However, don't try to spread yourself too thin or concentrate on working on multiple goals at the same time. So, take a couple of breaks, pace yourself, and don't be in a rush. Try to keep your goals simple and concentrate on only one thing at a time.

ESFP

This personality type is seldom interested in thinking about the future or in any long-term goals. It can become tricky to set goals for yourself if you cannot see the bigger picture. Before you set any goals, spend some time trying to think about your life. Thorough self-introspection is required to understand if you are on the right track or not.

ISFP

This personality type loves freedom, autonomy, and staying in the moment. Therefore, they might have a little trouble planning the future. Ensure that whenever you set goals, they are based on taking specific actions and behaviors. If the goals seem vague, abstract, or immaterial, you will quickly lose the motivation to stay on track.

ESTP

One of the biggest problems of this personality type is that they don't like the idea of sacrificing their lives in the present to work on carving a future for themselves. It is also one reason why they quickly abandon their goals if they interfere with their present life. This personality type thrives when there are short-term and practical goals. However, they like accomplishing things. So, whenever you set goals, ensure that the long-term goal is divided into several short-term goals.

ISTP

This personality type often sets vague goals. On the plus side, they are motivated to attain the goals they set for themselves. However, they always stick to a specific aspect of their lives. To succeed in life and an all-rounder, you must set goals in all aspects of your life and not just one. So, try setting those goals that you pursue outside your comfort zone while directing you toward excellence.

Note: remember that these are mere suggestions based on the dominant traits of various personality types. The goals you set for yourself boils down to your wants and desires in life.

Chapter Three: Why You Don't Need S.M.A.R.T (or Other Fancy) Goals

A SMART goal is a commonly-used acronym to define small, measurable, attainable, realistic, and time-bound goals. SMART goals are common, and it is perhaps the first thought that pops into your head when you think about setting goals. The primary idea behind SMART goals is to come up with small yet clearly defined goals that lend direction while establishing a specific timeframe to attain the said goals. It is believed this timeline helps overcome procrastination while motivating you to stay on track. So, it is safe to assume that these goals work exceptionally well while working toward attaining a well-defined target if everything else stays the same. When the target is realistic and the progress is well within your control, these goals provide short-term direction and enable you to plan for other long-term goals.

SMART goals aren't always the ideal fit. This goal cannot be blindly applied to all pursuits in life. Doing this is the perfect recipe for disaster. If you want to achieve ultimate greatness or are aiming for big dreams, especially in an ever-changing environment, these goals are inadequate and can be detrimental to success. SMART goals are based on the assumption that the person setting them has innate willpower and motivation to attain the said goals. It might not always be the case, and it is okay if you don't set SMART goals. So, you no longer need SMART goals to attain success.

Think about an important goal you achieved. Perhaps you successfully ran a marathon, lost all the excess weight you were carrying, or maybe made a career change. Now, ask yourself these questions.

- Was that achievement easy or difficult to attain?

- Did it take little or extra effort to attain that goal?

- Did you already know everything you needed when you started, or did you have to learn new skills along the way?

- Were you completely free from worry, or did you have a couple of doubts along the way?

So, what do these questions tell you about your history with any of the significant goals in life? You will realize that every notable accomplishment in your life resulted from a challenging goal. It required a lot of effort, was tricky, you probably had to learn something new, and might even have had moments of worry. All the noteworthy accomplishments of successful people were often difficult, requiring a lot of effort, depending on their ability to learn new skills, and even resulted in some nervousness.

Now, when you look at SMART goals, you will realize all that's stated above is quite the opposite of what SMART goals suggest. Steve Jobs used to say, "We are here to put a dent in the universe." Well, you cannot put a dent in the universe if you keep doing things entirely attainable. With SMART goals, it almost looks like it says, "Play it safe and stick within your limits." If you get stuck in your comfort zone, you cannot succeed. If you keep working to attain only the things you know you can do easily, you cannot discover true greatness. If every goal is realistic and attainable, then different inventions we see today like the Kindle, the Internet, the iPod, the Human Genome Project, etc., would not exist. SMART goals stifle creativity, and they aren't the key to dreaming big. If your dreams are confined to only things you can accomplish, you can never push yourself to your limits or even discover your true potential.

Fortunately, most of us have plenty of undiscovered potentials stored within. To get there, then you need challenging goals, and SMART goals will not work. In this section, let us look at some reasons SMART goals don't always work.

Measuring Success and Failure

While using the acronym SMART, the goal you set must be measurable and specific. These two criteria help objectively evaluate whether you have achieved a specific goal or not. This type of goal is quite useful while managing progress. However, their effectiveness is based on another factor: whether the environment you are working in is static or dynamic. SMART goals work only in a controllable environment. Therefore, applying this criterion to measure failure or success, especially in a dynamic or extreme environment, can be demotivating. Also, it might motivate you in the wrong direction. This outcome is potentially dangerous and detrimental to success.

By measuring success using SMART goals, you might end up where you are blindly pursuing your goals. You might not even realize why you are doing certain things, just because you are trying to accomplish your set goals. In such a situation, if you fail to meet a SMART goal, it can be quite demotivating. So, if your goal is to complete writing a 200-page book within a week, failing to meet this goal will essentially demotivate you. When you set this goal, you were probably sure that you could complete it. However, if you don't complete this within the set timeframe, you can feel lost. Because of this goal, you might not even be able to see the progress you have made. Instead of appreciating all that you have achieved, you will concentrate only on the objective you did not meet. So, the factor that gives you the motivation to keep going will send you into a tailspin when you don't achieve the established goals.

Narrows Your Focus

When you fixate all your attention only on one SMART goal, then you will ignore everything else. You might be so overcome by the need to attain this goal that it becomes your only priority. This fine-tuned approach to attaining a goal will work in a steady-state situation. Well, life is unpredictable, and it is improbable that factors that might influence your ability to attain the goal will always stay the same. In your bid to accomplish the SMART goal, you might overlook all the other opportunities that come along your way.

Giving Up Quickly

At times, SMART goals can be a little discouraging before or after attaining the goals. Were there times when you said, "I don't have the time to this," while excusing yourself for not doing something that you planned to do on a specific day? Well, the most popular application of the SMART goal is time management. Whenever it comes to time allocation for a specific task, it is usually in terms of all or nothing thinking. SMART goals are often viewed as a singular entity. So, if you cannot do something that you planned, it can be discouraging, and it might increase the **chances of abandoning the goal altogether.**

Low Goals

When you start using SMART goals to test whether your goals are the most effective or not, you are essentially encouraging yourself to set lower goals. Specific and measurable goals are ideal in certain situations, but usually, they produce results that lead to premature satisfaction or even reduced effort. For instance, let us assume that a salesperson sets a goal of increasing sales in his region by 5%. Now, he achieves this goal within the set timeframe. So, were he following SMART goals, then he would be happy about achieving this target. However, if the growth potential in that region could have been increased to 15%, he will not use his full potential. In this instance,

SMART goals lead to premature satisfaction. Also, he might lose enthusiasm to further increase sales since he has achieved a SMART goal.

Compromises

The first criterion in a SMART goal is that the goal must be specific. Setting a specific goal is effective. However, on the downside, there are inherent problems in setting specific goals. Perhaps the biggest trouble is, you might ignore the different factors that might help you attain your goals. For instance, during the 1970s, Ford manufactured Pintos to solely reduce the overall cost of the car to less than $2000. In their bid to do this, they cut corners. They compromised on safety and came up with a design that placed the gas tank in the car in a position that left it vulnerable in cases of collisions. It not only resulted in several claims against the company but also cost them their reputation. By using SMART goals, the company attained its objective of reducing the overall cost but ended up making a hefty compromise on the safety of the vehicle. Likewise, when you set SMART goals, you open up yourself for unnecessary compromises since your primary focus will be on a specific goal.

Can be Misleading

Before pursuing an achievable and realistic goal like concentrating on your next promotion, increasing your sales, or getting an award, ask yourself, "At what cost am I doing this?" You might not realize it, but you can easily overload yourself with several top priorities by setting SMART goals. A specific task is a top priority for a reason. So, when too many tasks vie for this position, the position itself becomes meaningless. Everything cannot occupy the number one position on your list of priorities.

When you observe every goal in isolation, it might seem achievable and realistic within a given timeframe. This might prompt you to become overly ambitious and believe that you can figure a way out and fit everything in your schedule. However, remember that "realistic" is a very relative term, and it is not absolute. It is not just about understanding whether a specific goal is realistic, given your capabilities, but also about understanding how realistic it is in relation to your other goals. You need to have a broad vision if you want to pursue lofty dreams and goals. SMART goals merely act as checkpoints, but they must not be the end goal.

Can Be Overwhelming

It can be a source of incredible stress if you are continually working toward attaining specific and time-bound goals. We already lead stressful lives and don't need any external or added stress. It can harm your health and even your overall lifestyle. Keep in mind that pursuing a long-term goal is not a short journey. It is something that you must keep doing consistently. It takes plenty of focus and energy. If you set SMART goals for yourself, you are merely increasing the stress you feel.

So, you no longer have to spend hours on end coming up with SMART goals. It is time to look for more effective and efficient techniques of goal setting.

Chapter Four: Your Mission, Vision, and Core Values

Usually, the terms vision and mission statement are used while describing the purpose of an organization. However, there is no reason why you cannot create your personal mission and vision statements.

So, you must be wondering why you need any of these statements. Well, words tend to have a certain power. When you don't have a precise long-term goal in your mind, you tend to become reactive instead of being proactive in life. Most of us usually concentrate on immediate or short-term goals whenever we make a decision. However, if you want to be successful, you must concentrate on the present and think about the future. A successful person knows this. It is one reason why most successful people often have their mission and vision statements in place.

While going through life, it is relatively easy to get overwhelmed by different mundane activities. When you have a vision statement on hand, it gives you a better idea of the future you wish to create for yourself. It also lends meaning to various activities you partake in. Apart from all this, these statements help determine your personal values and core principles that you would not want to compromise on.

When you have an idea of all this, it becomes easier to set goals for yourself *and accomplish the goals.* It lends a sense of balance to your life while preventing any burnout.

By having vision and mission statements, you can become more determined. It enables you to push yourself beyond your boundaries and step outside the comfort zone. Unless and until you do this, you cannot be successful. It enables you to build a life by design and not one that occurs by chance.

In this section, you will learn about the difference between a mission statement, vision statement, and core values. Even though all these three things sound quite similar, there are minute differences between them. Once you understand these differences, it becomes easier to establish goals for yourself. Apart from this, it will also give you better insight into yourself.

Vision Statement

A vision statement usually describes a specific dream; the organization wishes to achieve. It addresses the primary question, "What is the long-term goal of this organization?" Some of the popular vision statements of different companies are as follows.

- Ford Motors - To become the world's leading consumer company for automotive products and services.

- Disney - To make people happy.

- Amazon - Our vision is to be Earth's most consumer-centric company; to build a place where people can come to find and discover anything they want to buy online.

The definition of a vision statement that applies to a company is applicable on a personal level too. Your vision statement essentially describes one long-term goal that you wish to achieve in your life. It is also a true reflection of all the different values or characteristics that are dear to you. Here is an example of a personal vision statement, "I want to be a successful politician. It is my vision to inspire, motivate, and encourage people to live their lives to their fullest potential while contributing to society's development."

Mission Statement

A mission statement often describes how an organization wishes to attain its vision. The same rule applies to a personal mission statement too. It essentially addresses the question, "What can I do to attain your goals?" A vision statement deals with the future you want to carve for yourself.

On the other hand, a mission statement deals with the action you can take today to create the future. It provides a sense of direction and ensures that all your actions will bring you closer to your goal. It also prevents distractions from creeping in, which hinders your ability to concentrate on your goals.

Core Values

Your core values are different characteristic traits, beliefs, and principles that support your vision and mission statements. Some certain beliefs or principles are non-negotiable under any circumstances. They are quintessential for ensuring that your personal satisfaction stays high while you concentrate on attaining your goals. Different examples of core values include acceptance, logic, growth, safety, justice, knowledge, faith, passion, adventure, etc. Unless your goals align with your mission and vision statement, the chances of attaining them aren't high. If your goals contradict these things, you will quickly lose interest in them and might start procrastinating.

Steps to Follow

Here is a simple template you can follow in coming up with your mission statement. You don't have to spend hour's together brainstorming ideas. Start answering the questions as you go along, and within no time, you will have your personal mission statement. It doesn't take long to answer these questions, so set some time aside for it. Also, ensure that you are answering the questions as truthfully and honestly as you possibly can. After all, the aim is to develop your personal vision and mission statements.

Your Basic Characteristics

Here are various personal characteristics, and it is time to start prioritizing them from the most to the least important ones. If you think a characteristic is missing, feel free to add it to the list.

- Capable
- Broadminded
- Ambitious
- Dependable
- Cheerful
- Courageous
- Forgiving
- Friendly
- Honest
- Imaginative
- Helpful
- Intellectual
- Logical
- Independent
- Loving
- Organized
- Polite
- Obedient
- Innovative
- Self-confident
- Self-assured
- Self-controlled

What Are Your Values?

Here are various personal values, and it is time to start prioritizing them from the most to the least important ones. If you think something is missing, feel free to add it to the list. Carefully rank them because these values will act as guiding principles in your life.

- Creating a comfortable life
- Attaining personal and professional goals
- Leading an exciting life
- Living a happy life
- Desiring family security
- Peace of mind
- A sense of accomplishment
- Forming meaningful relationships
- Contributing to society
- A pleasurable life
- Spiritual salvation
- Leaving a legacy
- Happiness and independence

What is Important?

Carefully go through the ranking of the different personal characteristics and values you completed in the previous sections. Were there any values or characteristics that are important to you but weren't listed? If yes, then you merely need to add them to your list. Now, start rating them in their order of importance. Start listing out eight of your topmost values and characteristics. All these will be your core values and characteristics that you cannot swerve from in any situation.

- List your values
- List your characteristics

What Roles Do You Play?

We all tend to play different roles in life like that of a student, employee, son, daughter, grandparent, husband, wife, parent, manager, CEO, etc. Think about all the different roles you play and start describing the purpose you serve in a specific role. There are four specific questions you must answer while listing out the rules and your purpose in it. The questions are as follows.

- Why do you play this role?

- Why is this role important to you?

- Is there anyone who depends on you? If yes, then who depends on you?

- Who benefits from all these roles?

Note: Don't list out more than five roles.

How Do You Interact With Others?

You cannot get along in this world unless you get along with people and interact with them. There are various ways in which we successfully interact with others. In this section, it is time to list how you interact with others. Here are specific examples you can use. If something is missing from the list, please feel free to add on.

- Entertain
- Advice
- Reassure
- Teach
- Lead
- Manage
- Encourage
- Educate
- Love
- Stimulate

- Motivate

- Inspire

- Help

- Stud

- Plan

- Sell

- Provide

- Excite

- Support

- Serve

What About Awards?

- If you ever won an award, what would the award be for?

- How would you want the presenter to introduce you?

- What would your loved ones want to hear from you?

- What do you want in life?

- What do you want people to say about you after ten years?

- What do you want to accomplish in life?

- What experiences do you want to have?

- What do you want to own in life?

Time To Visualize

Now it is time to start visualizing your idea of a perfect world. What does your idea of a perfect world look like? Don't be judgmental, and allow your imagination to guide your way. Don't criticize yourself and merely make a mental note of all your thoughts. Once you do this, start listing out your idea of a perfect world.

Summing It All Up

Once you have completed all the different steps mentioned until now, you will better understand yourself. You will know your core values and basic characteristics. Combine all the concepts and words you picked up from the list of values, characteristics, roles, interactions, and things you want in life, along with your idea of a perfect world. When you combine all this, you'll be left with your mission statement. A simple example of a personal mission statement would be, "The purpose of my life is to use all the skills at my disposal to teach and motivate others to understand the journey in life and enjoy it."

Additional Tips

Your vision and mission statement must not exceed 50 words each. These statements must be easy to understand, concise, and reflect your true values and purpose. Also, don't fear making your vision statement bold. However, don't forget to be a little realistic. These statements must be in sync with your personal and professional goals. There are three crucial questions your vision and mission statements must address, and they are as follows.

- What are your passions in life?
- What are your core values?
- What sets you apart from the rest of the world?

Remember that a good vision statement often inspires you and pushes you to live your life to the fullest. It enables you to zero in on your passions and make the most of your skills and resources.

Once you have successfully created your vision and mission statements, don't forget to review them. Yes, they are usually long-term in nature, but it doesn't mean they are set in stone. As you go through life, different things will change. Therefore, your vision and mission statements must also change accordingly. Keep reviewing them and give yourself the required flexibility to modify them according to different circumstances. As you go along, there will be changes in your family life, job, career, health, and so on. Therefore, revise them at least once every year and try to accommodate all the changes.

Chapter Five: Pinpointing Your Goals with Why's and How's

Do you ever think about your personal reason for waking up every day? Unless you identify your purpose, it will become difficult to set any goals for yourself. In the previous chapters, you were given information about defining your vision statement, mission statement, and core values. However, these things will not hold any significant meaning to you unless you understand your reasons for setting goals. In this section, you'll learn about three simple steps you can follow to understand your purpose and identify the right goals along the way.

- Start by asking yourself "WHY" you want to attain specific goals.

- Now, ask yourself "HOW" you can implement your core values.

- It is time to ask yourself, "WHY" you must implement your core values.

Step #1: What is Your WHY?

Importance of Having a "WHY."

Unless you understand your purpose or "WHY," you cannot pursue things in life that give you absolute fulfillment, your reasons often serve as a point of reference for all the actions you take and decisions you make. It enables you to measure your progress and understand when you have attained your goals. There is a term in Japanese "ikigai" that translates to "a reason for being." Unless you know your purpose, you cannot make your life worthwhile.

When you understand your "WHY," it brings about a sense of clarity; if you ever noticed all people with a strong sense of purpose, they are often unstoppable. They have the power to shape their lives and live the way they want to. Likewise, when you have specific goals you wish to achieve and know your reasons for doing the same, you have a purpose every morning. If you don't know this purpose, you will waste your precious time and energy doing things that hold little or no meaning to you. Your purpose also ensures that you will follow up on your goals.

If you don't like settling for less, you must have a purpose you wish to work toward; when your passion fuels your goal, your chances of success increase. It also ensures that you stay focused on all the goals you have established. When you know what truly matters to you in life, you can dedicate your limited resources to those things. It is also a great way to de-clutter your life. If you are unaware of what is important, you might expend your limited energy on unnecessary clutter.

Setbacks are quite common in life. Unless you have a strong sense of purpose for attaining a specific goal, you cannot overcome setbacks. A lack of purpose will make you view a setback as the end of the road. A setback is merely an opportunity to learn and grow. You cannot think like this only when you have a strong sense of purpose. Therefore, your "WHY" enables you to develop resilience. Resilience allows you to bounce back from adversities.

When you know your purpose and understand what matters to you, you can hold onto your values. Therefore, having and understanding your reasons for attaining a goal enables you to live your life with integrity. When you follow your core values and stick to your primary characteristics, you will feel more satisfied with yourself and your life.

Steps to Find Your "WHY."

Now that you understand the importance of your "WHY," it is time to find your "WHY."

Make a list of all the activities you used to enjoy but don't indulge in anymore. When having fun, time certainly passes more quickly. So, it is time for a little self-introspection to identify your passions. Unless you are passionate about your goals, you cannot attain them. When you follow your passions, you can ensure that all your energy, time, and resources are spent working on something that lends meaning to your life. Another simple way to do this is to remember all the things you used to do in your childhood just because it was fun. As you go down memory lane, you might notice specific patterns or trends in activities you enjoy. Think about it for a moment, and these patterns hold clues to your real purpose in life.

Most adults often lose touch with various things they loved as children. Sadly, in adulthood, most of us falsely believe we must do things only when we are rewarded for them. This transactional nature of existence imbibed into us by societal norms can make anyone feel dejected. Therefore, it is time to put a stop to all this and understand your passions.

In sync with the previous step, it is time to think about all the things you would want to do in life, even if it made you look like a fool. Before you can excel at something, there will; be some point you stumble and fall because of a lack of competence and knowledge. You cannot keep working on something even after embarrassing yourself for making mistakes unless you are passionate about it. Unless the activity at hand is meaningful to you, you will give up at the first sign of trouble. So, think about things you wouldn't shy away from, even if it means feeling foolish or silly.

Now, it is time to understand your talents. Not a lot of us know all our talents. Most of us brush away our talents because they don't seem worthy of societal acceptance. A simple way to understand yourself better is by noticing what others ask of you when they need your help.

You might not be able to see your talents how others do. For instance, you might not realize that you are inspiring your siblings, colleagues, or friends to be more like you. What is one thing your friends always thank you for? Do they come to you for advice? Do you serve as a sounding board? Another simple way to do this is by asking your loved ones about what they think your strengths are. Identifying your strengths can also enable you to find your passion in life. Once you identify your passion, setting goals becomes more manageable.

No one likes thinking about death. No one likes believing life is short, and most of us avoid these thoughts. Even if it sounds morose, it is time for critically analyzing your life. What would you do if you knew you just had a year to live? Would you keep living the life you are living right now? Or would you want to make any changes? We are all used to thinking, "I can do this later." However, what would you do if you knew that you just had a year to do everything you ever wanted and wished for? It helps put things in perspective and give you a better understanding of yourself. It will also give you a better sense of purpose.

The best way to determine your purpose in life is by identifying things you can do to enrich others' lives. It would help if you had a certain degree of self-awareness to do this. When you are grateful for the life you live and contribute toward others' wellbeing, you will be more satisfied with yourself. It, in turn, will give you a strong sense of purpose.

What are the different things in life for which you wouldn't mind going the extra mile? There will be things you would want to keep making an effort even after facing setbacks and failures. Many people fail to realize that passion is only the result of action instead of causing it. If you are complacent, you can never find your passion in life. Finding your passion is a process of trial and error. If you're not willing to go out of your way for something, then it means you're not passionate about it.

To sum it all up, here are questions you must answer to find your "WHY."

- What do you love the most?

- What means the most to you in life?

- What would you want to do if you just had a year to live?

- What would you go out of your way for?

- What are the different activities you enjoy?

- What can you do to enrich the lives of those around you?

- What is the one thing you would love to do even if you get no monetary returns from it?

Step #2: How to Implement Your Core Values

Once you have identified your "WHY," it is time to work on your core values. Unless you implement your core values in your daily life, you cannot become successful. Your core values serve as a homing beacon. They help you identify any opportunities that come along your way while avoiding any trouble. In this section, let us look at simple tips you can follow to implement your core values.

You can revisit the previous chapter to understand your core values once again. They usually are single words or simple phrases. Once you have a list of your top 10 core values, write them down on post-its, and you can place them in your home. You can also digitize them and use them as screensavers, the home screen on your desktop, or place it anywhere else where you will see it daily. When you keep glancing at it daily, this message gets embedded in your mind.

Another great way to ensure that your core values always stay in your mind is by discussing them with your loved ones. When your close circle knows your core values and regularly discusses them, these values get stuck in your subconscious. It also enables them to get a better understanding of you as an individual.

The company you keep matters a lot. Regardless of your age, your company defines your personality. You might not realize it, but a great way to manage your core values is by managing the company you keep. It doesn't mean that everyone you spend the time that must share your core values. It merely means they must fit in it. For instance, if one of your core values is creativity, it doesn't mean you have to keep looking for all those individuals who are equally creative. However, it does mean you need people around you who support your creative approach in life. Instead of bringing you down or causing conflict, your support system must encourage you. When you spend time with ambitious, happy, successful people (and all things desirable), their positive traits will positively affect you. Likewise, spending time with negative company will negatively affect you.

Your core values will enable better decision-making. Put aside a couple of minutes in the morning to list all the tasks you wish to accomplish during the day. Once you have listed all the tasks, use your core values to gauge whether the tasks at hand are important for you or not. For instance, if your core value is impact, go through your list of tasks and weed out all those tasks that don't meet this core value. You'll probably want to do all those tasks that help maximize your results, but with minimum effort. Everything you do must follow who you are. When you do this, it becomes easier to attain your goals while maintaining your personal satisfaction.

When you integrate your core values into regular conversations, they take on a whole new meaning altogether. Even casually speaking about these core values allows you to express yourself. It is also a great way to be consistent while thinking about your core values. By making a part of your regular vocabulary, you get a chance to remind yourself of all you are and what you want to do in life without overlooking or forgetting it.

Not everyone is motivated to accomplish their goals. It is true when the goals you have set for yourself are not something that you're passionate about. Therefore, it is time to use your core values as motivators. They help determine the future you want to have. Every opportunity you get and the goals you set must be based on your core values. Unless they agree on your core values, they result in unnecessary internal conflict.

To keep improving yourself, then you need to spend some time for self-introspection. Take some time and think about all the different tasks you accomplished. Give yourself a moment to understand whether the day that went by you was in tune with your core values or not. If you notice any discrepancies, you can take corrective action to ensure that you get back on track the following day.

Step #3: Revisit Your "WHY"

The final step is to revisit your "WHY." Now, it is time to question yourself about why you must implement your core values. When you go through the different questions in this section, you will realize that your core values go back to your goals. Once your goals and core values are in sync, it becomes easier to take action, stay on track, and attain the goals.

What is Your Purpose?

• The first step to ensuring that the goals you set for yourself are right for you is by asking yourself these questions.

• Why do you want to attain this goal?

• Is this goal something you want to pursue, or do you feel like you must pursue it?

• What is the core value in your life this goal caters to?

If you feel like you are forced to pursue a goal, it is not the right one. If you have set a goal you wish to pursue, keep reminding yourself why it is important.

What is Your Idea of Success?

Start with the end result and visualize that you have attained your goals. Now, think back and list out the major milestones that helped you reach your destination. By doing this, you can identify any possible obstacles you might come across while working toward your ultimate goal. It essentially helps you avoid any roadblocks or obstacles, and instead, concentrate on attaining your goals.

What Will Your Life Look Like Once You Have Attained Your Goals?

Besides the previous question, try to think about any of the additional questions you can ask yourself to clarify the things you wish to achieve in life. What are your values? Are your goals in sync with your values? Is the goal something you honestly want, or are you trying to live up to someone else's expectations? The more questions you ask yourself, the closer will you be to the right answer. Unless the goal you have set for yourself is the right one, your chances of attaining it are slim.

What is Your Superpower?

The ability to question yourself is nothing short of a superpower. Unfortunately, not many first understand its true meaning and don't use this power at all. The best way to ensure that you are heading in the right direction is to question your chosen direction. So, who are you? By answering this question, you will have a real sense of your purpose and meaning in life. Besides this, it also gives you a better understanding of your core values and the goals you have set for yourself. Besides all this, it also helps determine whether the goal you set is the right one or not. Unless your goals go back to your core values, you cannot work to succeed.

Why Did You Choose the Goal?

Will this goal change any aspect of your life? If yes, then why will this goal bring about the said change? The chances of succeeding improve when you question yourself about all the things you do in life. When you know why you are doing something, the goal becomes more straightforward and less ambiguous. If your goal is vague, then the results will be vague too. It might even make you feel like you are a failure because of all this vagueness. So, try eliminating this by asking yourself why you chose a specific goal.

What Is It That You Wish To Achieve Ultimately?

The primary idea of this question is to help identify your goals and concentrate on taking actionable steps for attaining that goal. Once you know what you want in life or different aspects of your life, you can easily develop a plan of action that leads you to the most successful outcome. Every step you take in the present and the future must align with and be a part of the bigger picture. Unless you see the bigger picture, you cannot take these steps.

What Is Your Ideal Job Description?

Most of us know all the things we don't like about our job or art lives. When we know these things, we continuously try running away from them. Instead of doing this, think about the things you like. What is your ideal job description? Once you answer this, then you have a goal you can work toward. Instead of running away from it, you can run toward the goal you want to achieve. It also enables you to stop concentrating on the pain points and work on taking steps toward your ideal job description. It ensures that you are working in the right direction.

What Are Your Values?

You will be investing plenty of your resources to attain a goal. Your goal is closely associated with your core values. Unless you have clarity about your core values, you cannot attain your goals. Concentrate on things important to you and in-line with your goals. It helps reduce any distractions while improving your chances of success. Besides this, it is also rather fulfilling when you work on things you value in life.

What Keeps You Going In Life?

To identify whether the goal you have set for yourself is the right one or not, you must start by understanding yourself. Until you know what keeps you going in life, it will become challenging to determine whether you are headed in the right direction or not. Therefore, start by understanding who you are and where you wish to go from there. Then, question yourself about why you want to do a specific thing and what you can achieve by working toward the goal.

What Do Your Loved Ones Say About Your Goal?

Even when you are confident of the things you love in life, it doesn't hurt to get a second opinion. Remember that you are merely consulting and not seeking the answers to your questions from others. You can always ask your trusted friends, family members, partner, or anyone you love to share their opinions about what they feel about your goals. It helps improve your self-awareness. Also, they might see certain opportunities and obstacles you are oblivious to. Additional information always comes in handy.

Chapter Six: Nine Lazy Goal-Setting Hacks

Are there days when you feel incredibly inspired to get your life organized? It could be a random burst of motivation at three in the morning or a constant urge to get it together after a motivating day at work. Well, if yes, then you are like the rest of us. However, there is only one small problem with this entire thing: the lack of motivation. You might experience a random burst of motivation, but you don't always feel motivated to set and work toward attaining goals. So, how can you set goals when you feel a little lazy or low on motivation? Well, in this section, you'll learn about specific practical tips you can follow to get things done quite easily.

Tip #1: Always Start Small

When you're trying to work toward a goal, start with something small. It could be a small step, but it still counts. For instance, if your goal is to get a promotion at work, it is an important goal. This goal might seem complicated and even overwhelm you. Instead of concentrating on getting promoted, concentrate on turning in all your work on time. Let others see you are dependable and punctual. Don't forget to deliver on your promises, and whenever possible, turn in the work earlier than expected. Within no time, your boss will notice the effort you make. Break down the primary goal into smaller steps you can work on. This works exceptionally well when running low on motivation.

It might sound like a SMART goal idea, but it works. However, ensure that the goal you are working toward is something you genuinely care for.

Tip #2: Talk to Others

There might be someone in your circle - a friend, family member, colleague, or acquaintance who always seem put-together and confident. If there is a go-getter in your circle, then it is time to talk with that person. Ask the person for some advice you can incorporate into your daily life and routine. You probably need not follow all the methods the other person uses, but it probably gives you better insight into the things that work and doesn't. In fact, don't merely try to copy or replicate the other person's behavior without understanding what you wish to accomplish. You might end up with some practical advice you can use to develop the kind of attitude required for succeeding.

Tip #3: Start Yesterday

If your motivation levels don't run high, or if you are not usually a motivated individual, then procrastination creeps in. Once procrastination gets hold of you, getting anything done will become incredibly difficult. Procrastination can get to the best of us. However, unless you stop procrastinating and take some action, you get nothing done. So, it is time to get started soon. Stop telling yourself, "now is not the right time," "I will do it tomorrow," or "this can wait." If you keep telling yourself these things, remember that you are merely making excuses. You are procrastinating and are putting off something until a later date, which can be done right now. If you wait, you cannot attain whatever you want. If that's not an option, then it is time to get started ASAP. If you notice procrastination creeping in while you are trying to do something, then remind yourself you were supposed to start it yesterday itself! Time is precious, and once it goes back, you cannot get it back. So, stop wasting it and concentrate on getting things done.

Tip #4: Concentrate On Your Likes

Always concentrate on doing the things we love and forget about the rest. It might sound like a piece of advice that is easier said than done. Regardless of how much you love something, you cannot afford to forget about everything else in your life. For instance, just because you're working on a goal you desire doesn't mean you can do away with your other responsibilities like going to the grocery store, maintaining dentist appointments, and keeping up with different commitments. However, if you set a goal for yourself, then you must follow your heart and ensure there is sufficient time for it. The best way to do this is by ensuring that your goal resonates with your core values. Once you like the direction you are headed in, it becomes easier to make the required effort.

Tip #5: Understand Yourself

Accountability matters a lot when it comes to setting and attaining goals. It matters even more if you are running low on motivation or feel a little lazy. When you hold yourself accountable, not just to yourself but to others, it increases your motivation to keep going. Even when you have no motivation, the mere fact that others will hold you accountable for attaining the goal will give you the motivation to take the required action. So, whenever you set a major life goal, you can post about it on social media or talk to your close circle about it. By doing this, you are essentially telling others what you want to accomplish while making yourself more responsible for your goals. Also, it always helps to have a support system in place. Once your close circle understands what you're doing and why you are doing it, they will stand by you and give you the motivation they require on the days when you have none!

Tip #6: Not Accomplishing the Goal

At times, we all need a reality check to get started and keep moving. For attaining your goals, concentrating on the idea of success is a good idea. However, it doesn't always work. Instead, try picturing how your life would be if you don't accomplish your goals. Concentrate on how you would feel and what you would be missing out on. Concentrate on all the negative emotions associated with not attaining the goals. These negative emotions might scare you a little. Well, this is precisely what you need to keep going. A little fear is a great motivation and energy booster. The next time you don't want to work on something, remind yourself of how you would feel when you don't accomplish the goal.

Tip #7: Be Honest

Don't work on a goal merely because society tells you to or because someone in your close circle tells you to. The goal must be ideal for you, and it is time to ensure that you are not living someone else's dreams. If you are confident that you are genuinely excited and happy about something you're doing – and not just listening to those around you – then you are on the right path. If you keep doing things to please others or because others believe it is a good idea, you will never find the motivation to get things done.

Tip #8: Mini-Goals

Do you ever feel like getting someplace instead of being stuck on the side of the road, wondering how long it would take until you finally reach your destination? If this ever happens to you or has happened to you, then you'll realize it zaps out motivation. If you feel like you are not making progress, you will not want to work on it. The same stands true when you cannot see the progress you make. So, to avoid all this, it is time to set some mini-goals for yourself. Instead of getting overwhelmed, thinking about a big goal you want to achieve, concentrate on the mini-goals. For instance, if you are trying to get a promotion, then maybe you can start by getting your boss to approve one of your new ideas or maybe even spend some time connecting with your coworkers. These are relatively simple and achievable. Achievable goals will help you accomplish what seemed unattainable initially.

Tip #9: Don't Forget to Have Fun

You must put in plenty of effort to meet a specific goal. However, it doesn't mean there isn't a reason you cannot enjoy the process. If you don't enjoy doing all this, then what is the point? Even if it sounds like a cliché, meeting every challenge with a smile on your face changes the way things work out for you. Your attitude matters a lot in life. If you stay positive, understand the process, and have fun along the way, attaining goals will become more effortless.

By now, you would have realized that setting goals are not just for determined and motivated individuals. Anyone can set goals. However, the one aspect of goal setting you must not overlook is the way you set goals. If you set goals that cannot be attained or don't try to attain the goals, you will merely disappoint yourself.

Chapter Seven: Mind-Mapping for Clarity

What is Mind-Mapping?

Mind mapping is the graphic representation that helps connect information about a central topic. It is almost like a tree, where the main idea represents the trunk, and all the associations drawn from it are like the branches of a tree. In mind mapping, you can use words, pictures, or even symbols to represent your ideas and goals. Mind mapping is not a new concept, and it has been around for centuries now. Great thinkers like Leonardo da Vinci, Albert Einstein, Darwin, and even Edison used various visual representation methods to express their ideas.

The idea of mind mapping was popularized by Tony Buzan, a popular educator, author, and psychologist. To improve his ability to analyze and retain information while in college, he came up with specific keywords and phrases, adding color to essential concepts, forming associations by drawing lines, and then adding boxes to the relevant text. While doing this, he realized that the usual notes' information was noticeably less than the ones present in a mind map.

Mind mapping can be used for brainstorming, managing meetings, decision-making, organizing information, strategic thinking, improving work productivity, and even event planning. Not only students but people in many other age groups can utilize mind maps.

What Are the Benefits of Mind-Mapping?

Now that you're aware of what mind mapping means, let us look at the benefits it offers.

One of the significant benefits of mind mapping is the speed at offers. When you no longer have to write sentences and paragraphs, you can save plenty of time. All this time you saved can be used for something more creative. By merely noting down a phrase or word, you can understand the meaning of an entire sentence or paragraph. It comes in handy, especially while dealing with complicated topics, by noting down key words –or even symbols – you cut down on all the time. You might have spent making notes. It also enables your mind to form associations quickly.

Mind mapping helps improve your creativity because it emphasizes brainstorming, the formation of associations, and gradient thinking. Unlike a computer, your brain cannot function linearly, at least not all the time. Whenever you read any information, your brain undertakes various functions like comparison, integration, and synthesis of all your thoughts. Most of these mental functions rely on associations. Words are merely a verbal representation of an idea you have in your head. When you link a word to a specific idea, it helps uncover other ideas stored within. When you think about a specific topic in this manner, you might come up with various subcategories you didn't know existed, and your mind keeps forming associations all this time. It helps obtain a fresh perspective when looking at certain things in life.

A mind map is a thorough visual representation of all your ideas and thoughts in one place. Instead of going through plenty of text, you merely need to look at a mind map to get a bird's eye view of a specific topic. Processing information and understanding the same in this manner becomes easy. Also, since it is free from clutter, you save yourself plenty of trouble of having to read through a topic. Besides this, mind-mapping also allows you to look at different associations between various topics carefully.

When you start forming associations, it becomes easier for your mind to retain information. It, in turn, improves your memory. Whenever you write something down either physically on the paper or type it out on your computer, it gets stored in your memory. It is an effective way of learning when compared to reading. Mind maps are not readily available, and it takes a little effort to make them. This conscious effort you make means it is easier for your brain to remember all the information.

Since all the information and associations are represented visually, it lends a better sense of clarity. It not only offers a brief explanation or synopsis, but it ensures that you have better clarity of the subject too. A mind map doesn't encourage clattering of information, so your brain can quickly zero in on the essential concepts. Mind mapping is also a great way to brainstorm new ideas. Whenever you feel like you have hit a wall, start mind mapping. Sometimes, all it takes is to place your idea on paper or on the computer screen to help you come up with different answers to a problem.

Steps to Follow

Mind mapping is a great technique that enables you to divide your goals into smaller ones. When you make this division, you will have a better understanding of all you wish to attain. A mind map gives you a visual representation of all the small goals you can take to attain those goals in different steps. You can see all this with no excessive clutter, making it easier to understand the ideal course of action.

The first step is to collect your goals. Essentially, it means you must note different keywords or small sentences that represent your goals. Spend some time and write everything down until you cannot come up with more ideas. In this stage, you are merely dumping all your ideas on a piece of paper, and selection comes next. On a sheet of paper, write down the central theme- goals.

The next step is to start forming general associations around the central theme. For instance, the different general associations associated with goals could be various aspects of your life, like personal, professional, social, financial, or even educational. Now, go back to the list of goals you made in the previous step and segregate them according to different aspects of your life. Once you have segregated them, it is time to note all the concerned goals next to the general associations in the mind map. Once you have completed this step, you can notice different branches flowing from the central theme to different categories of goals and the subcategories in each area.

Ensure that you don't include over three goals for a specific aspect of your life. If there are more goals than this and become cluttered, the chances of getting distracted will increase. Here is a simple example of how a mind map can look. Instead of noting them in bullet points, you can place them next to one another with the central theme in the center of the page. From the central theme, draw lines until you reach the desired area of your life. It will essentially look like a cobweb spreading out in different directions. Every line you extend will merely increase the area that the web covers. You can make the mind map as detailed as you want. Under this, you can also write down the reasons for working on a specific goal and the course of action you can take to attain the goals. Use different colors to make the mind map more attractive and highlight the critical aspects of your life. However, your work doesn't, and once you have created a mind map. The mind map merely serves as a reminder of all that you wish to accomplish. So, you must put in the required effort and spend the time necessary to attain those goals.

Goals

1. Personal

a. Playing a sport you enjoy

b. Spending more time with your loved ones

c. Eating healthy and wholesome meals

2. Professional

a. Learning a specific job-related skill

b. Working for a promotion

c. Applying for new jobs

3. Social

a. Going out twice a week

b. Spending more time with friends

c. Plan a family holiday

If you don't like the idea of manually drawing a mind map, you can use online software to do this. The best mind mapping software available in the market these days is as follows.

- MindMeister
- LucidChart
- Cacoo
- Mindomo
- XMind
- MindManager
- Canava
- Padlet
- Mind Genius
- Mindmap
- Coggle

Chapter Eight: The Power of Vision Boards

What is a Vision Board?

The law of attraction states that your general attitude and beliefs in life tend to act like a magnet that attracts different circumstances, events, and opportunities that allow you to live out all those beliefs and attitudes. The law of attraction is a compelling suggestion that provides an opportunity to shape your life by attracting and manifesting your deepest desires. One of the best ways to leverage the power of the law of attraction is by creating a vision board.

A vision board is more than merely cutting and pasting different magazine cutouts and pictures on a sheet of paper or board. It is a simple tool that helps consciously remind you of your goals and dreams. A vision board is also known as a dream board, and it helps narrow down all your true desires through the power of choice. If you want to vision board to work, then it must clearly show the life you wish to lead. It can include magazine cutouts, images, inspirational quotes, or anything else you want to include. A conventional vision board is made by taking different cutouts of images and texts from magazines or any other printed media onto a corkboard, poster, or a sturdy board of your choice. If you don't like the idea of spending time creating a vision board like this, then you can use various online applications to do the same. You will learn about all these things in this section.

Benefits of a Vision Board

Zero In On a Goal

So, how does a vision board work? The power of choice, visualization, and consistency are the three critical ingredients upon which a vision board's power rests. A vision board forces you to understand and examine all your desires. It enables you to concentrate only on the goals that matter the most to you. This simple process of choosing what you wish to put on the vision board is meaningful. Start by identifying your deepest desires and then selecting images, pictures, and text representing those desires. For instance, if your dream is to purchase a house, then you might place a picture of a house on the vision board. However, if you are unhappy with pasting just one image, you can find various representations of your dreams and make a collage of all the kinds of houses you like and paste it on the vision board.

Makes You Believe

By focusing on the small details, your mind is forced to analyze things that matter the most to you carefully. The power of visualization can never be underestimated. This board's visual aspect is the primary factor that helps drive home the message about your desires. When you start visualizing, concentrate on all the little details associated with your goal. Concentrate on the feelings, emotions, surroundings, external environment, the way your body feels, and everything else you can think of. When you do it right, the act of visualization is almost as powerful as performing the act itself. It helps you focus on the things you desire and then fills you with positive energy and motivation required to keep going. A vision board helps you realize your dream in your mind, so you believe it is possible to accomplish that dream.

Brings About Consistency

Consistency is essential in life, and it is quintessential for attaining success. Whether or not you are trying to form a new habit, work on your goals, or learn a new skill, you need consistency. The human brain is wired for repetition. Whenever you repeat an action, the said action becomes more robust and more refined. Create a vision board and place it in a place such that you can see it daily. By consistently visualizing your goals, you are training yourself to manifest your deepest desires.

Steps to Follow

Step 1: Start Planning

The first step is to plan the kind of vision board you wish to create. Think about the message your personalized vision board must convey and how you want it to look. You must ask yourself some questions before you can create a vision board, and they are as follows.

What are your goals or desires you want the vision board to reflect?

The different areas of your life you can consider while setting a goal are your values, career, family, love, life, health, and wellness. You can also think about how you would want to spend your free time or think about the life you want to lead.

Do You Want to Create a Single Board or Multiple Boards?

Some like creating small boards for visualizing different categories of their streams, while others prefer making one large board that includes everything they desire. Remember that regardless of the vision board's size, you must place it such that you can look at it daily. So, consider the space available.

What Are the Different Types of Images You Want to Use?

Do you want to print out images? Do you want to use any photographs you have at hand? Do you want to cut out images and pictures from magazines or any other print media? You can also print pictures from your Pinterest board or any quotes from the Internet. Besides this, you can stick pages from a book, flyers, brochures, and pamphlets on the vision board. The sky is the limit with a vision board.

How Do You Want the Vision Board to Look?

Do you want the vision board to look messy or tidy? Some people like their vision board to be crowded and cluttered with different things, while others prefer to look tidy and neat. Once again, it is up to you. You can also add various decorative elements to this board. You can also think about placing certain crystals or even burning some soothing incense near the vision board. Crystals can be charged with your intentions, and they also help manifest the law of attraction. You can use helpful crystals like clear quartz, amethyst, sapphire, rose quartz, tourmaline, citrine, and so on to strengthen your vision board.

Step #2: Gather Supplies

Once you have decided about all the different things you want to include in and around the vision board, it is time to gather all the supplies you require. It might take you a little while to gather all the images, pictures, quotes, or anything else you want to add to the vision board. Remember that you can always keep adding onto the vision board. You need not make it perfect on the first attempt. You can also write quotes on the vision board that inspire you.

Step #3: Get Started

Now that you have everything ready, it is time to get started. While creating a vision board, find a quiet spot for yourself. You can also play some calming and soothing music in the background while burning from incidents. All these things help calm your mind and enable you to think about your dreams and goals. Before you start, you can meditate for a while or send out a silent prayer to the universe to help you. You are seeking the energy of the universe to help you here. So, sending out a prayer might be helpful.

Step #4: Using the Vision Board

The vision board can express a literal, complicated, or metaphorical story. As long as it is the accurate representation of your deepest desires, the story can be expressed in any way. Ensure that everything you put on the vision board mirrors your goals and aspirations of life. So, whenever you look at this board, thoughts about your goals and aspirations must immediately come to your mind. Once you have created the vision board, it is time to use it. Don't forget to place this vision board at your home such that you see it every day. You can place it on your nightstand or any other place you want. Place it such this vision board is the first thing you look at as soon as you wake up in the morning and the last thing before you go to sleep at night. Make it a point to set for about 10 minutes with your vision board at least once or twice a week. Visualize all the goals you want to achieve in life. This visualization will give you the motivation and energy you require to keep going.

Digital Vision Boards

If you like arts and crafts or DIY projects, you can make the vision board at home. It hardly takes an hour or two to make the vision board. However, if you are running short of time or don't like indulging in DIY projects, you can always choose a digital version. You can create a digital vision board using online software or applications. A great thing about a digital vision board is that you can easily access it anywhere since you can carry its softcopy with you.

Most of the online software or applications offer a massive database of inspiring photographs, quotes, and themes you can use to set up the vision board. You don't have to sit and collect these supplies; merely use the resources available online. The different vision board applications and websites to turn your dreams into reality are as follows.

- DreamItAlive
- Visuapp
- Corkulous Professional
- iWish
- MindMovies
- Canva
- Hay House Vision Board

Chapter Nine: Goals and Time Management

Managing your time wisely is probably the most powerful skill that can take you places in life. Time management helps you in different life stages and isn't just confined to your professional life. If you are not using your time wisely, the chances are slim that you will ever reach your goals or even get anything done. One thing that is constant for everyone regardless of their age, sex, geographical location, or any other demographic factor is how time passes by: time doesn't wait for anyone, and if you keep squandering this precious resource away, you will never get to your destination. We all have precisely 24-hours or 86,400 seconds in a day. Regardless of what you might want to or wish to believe, this is all the time you must work with. The way you organize your daily schedule and utilize your time matters a lot when it comes to attaining your goals.

So, what is time management? Time management is a simple process of planning and organizing how you divide all the time available to you daily for different activities. Time management ensures that you are not only working harder but smarter too. It helps you accomplish more in less time. Time management improves your overall efficiency and productivity, helps build your reputation, reduces stress, opens up different opportunities, and helps you succeed in life. Remember that being busy differs from being productive. Unless you are productive and engage in activities that bring you a step closer to your goal, you are merely wasting your time.

The inability to effectively prioritize, procrastination, and unrequited laziness are among the leading factors for improper time management. Regardless of the goals you have set for yourself, you cannot attain them if you don't learn to manage your time effectively. In this section, let us look at some simple tips you can follow to attain your goals using time management.

Tip #1: Existing Routine

To become better at managing your time, then you must become aware of your current routine. Spend some time and think about the way you spend your time daily. You can maintain a journal. However, these days there are plenty of task reminders and to-do list apps you can use to track the time spent. Think about the last ten days and notice how you spend your time. You can immediately identify patterns. For instance, you might realize that your productivity is high in the morning while it reduces around the evening. So, you can schedule the most important tasks early in the morning and reduce your burden toward the evening. By optimizing the time available and concentrating on essential tasks, you can accomplish more.

Tip #2: Start Prioritizing

To be successful, and wish to accomplish your goals in life, then you must start prioritizing. We all have plenty of things that take away our attention. So, unless you concentrate on the things that matter, you get nothing done. The best way to prioritize your tasks is by completing the most critical and daunting tasks before moving onto anything else.

Here is a sample of the time management matrix. In this matrix, you must divide a paper into four parts. Each quadrant represents a specific task or set of tasks. The four quadrants are as follows.

Tasks that are important and urgent: All these tasks are important and require your immediate attention. They have a high urgency rate and must be completed within a deadline. Get to these tasks right away.

Tasks that are important but not urgent: All these tasks are important, but they are not urgent. So, you can put them on hold for a while. They don't need your immediate attention, but it doesn't mean you forget about them. To improve your ability to manage your time, then concentrate on all the tasks that fall under this category.

Tasks that are not important but are urgent: There will be specific tasks that are quite urgent but are not necessary. You can easily delegate, minimize, or even eliminate these tasks since they don't contribute toward any of your goals.

Tasks that are not important and not urgent: These tasks offer little or no value altogether. They don't help you attain your goals. These tasks merely drain out your time and energy. Whenever you place specific tasks in this category, it is time to eliminate them. Try eliminating these tasks as much as you can to do more things.

Tip #3: Understand Your Goals

Ensure that the goal you have set is the right one for you. This step has been mentioned several times until now because it is quite vital. If the goal you set is not the right one for you, then you can never succeed. Instead of setting yourself up for disappointment, it is time to rewire the way you think. Understand your goals and your reasons for attaining them. Whenever in doubt, revisit the steps and tips discussed in previous chapters to understand your goals better.

Tip #4: Time Limits

A simple way to ensure that you make most of the 24 hours available at your disposal is by setting time limits for all the tasks you engage in throughout the day. Reading and replying to emails can be time-consuming. However, it must not be the only task you complete within the 24 hours available. When you assign specific time limits for specific tasks, you can manage your time instead of allowing the tasks to guide your daily routine. For instance, if you have set an hour aside to read and respond to emails, then do things within that hour. If it exceeds the time limit, then move on to the next task. Once you have completed all the other tasks you planned, you can go back to any task left unfinished. By doing this, you can ensure that you are completing all your tasks wasting no time.

Tip #5: Planning Ahead

In the previous steps, you were shown how you could prioritize different tasks at hand. Once you know your priorities, it is time to start planning. Spend some time and think about all the activities you must complete and how you want to complete them. It takes up a little time, but it is time well spent. You can make a to-do list, set a plan of action, or even set specific goals for the days to come. Usually, we all get caught up in mundane activities and daunting tasks we forget about planning. If you are unsure how to plan duties, you can do this either early in the morning or before you go to bed.

Before you sleep at night, spend some time and take a couple of minutes to clear your head. Once you feel calm, make a list of all the tasks you want to accomplish on the following day. When the list is ready, prioritize them in the order of their importance. So, as soon as you wake up in the morning, you will have an idea of all the important tasks you must complete before attending to anything else. It helps improve your overall productivity while giving you a better sense of purpose. Also, you will feel satisfied when you complete all the critical tasks within the given timeframe. If you don't want to do this at night, you can make up in the morning and set a couple of minutes aside to do this before working on anything else.

Tip #6: Walk Away

Keep trying and pushing yourself. However, you must also know when to stop and where to draw the line. It is okay to abandon a sinking ship instead of sinking with it. Walk away from any tasks, projects, or activities you know are headed toward an unfortunate destination. If they are headed nowhere, there is no point in wasting any of your time, energy, effort trying to complete them. It is OK to move on from an unproductive task toward something more productive. It is acceptable to know where you must spend your energy. If a specific task doesn't turn out the way you thought it would. Even after making all the possible effort, stop beating yourself up. Instead, realize that the time you have invested has passed you by. Learn the lesson; life is trying to teach you, and move on. , you can probably avoid making the mistakes you made in the past.

Tip #7: Say No

You are the only one who can decide what is right for you. If something doesn't feel right, or if you do want to do something, you can say no. Don't be under any misconceptions that you'll come across as being selfish if you say no. Learning to say no is a skill that comes in handy in all aspects of your life. Learning to say no is also quintessential for time management. Remember, you are the boss, and no one else can tell you otherwise.

If you have an important deadline or something urgent, you must work on it, then prioritize your own work. Don't go out with your friends or help a colleague when you are flooded with work. Do things, and then concentrate on the other things. It is more important to attend to the issues that matter for moving toward your own goals instead of focusing on what others need. Therefore, prioritize your needs and concentrate on getting things done. Sometimes, you cannot say no. In such instances, delegate work. Once you delegate your responsibilities to someone else, stop thinking about it and don't try to micromanage if you cannot say no, you will never learn how to manage all the time available to you effectively.

Tip #8: Start Decluttering

Decluttering is all about getting rid of clutter. When you work in an environment filled with unnecessary clutter, you lose focus and lose track of the task at hand. It is one reason why you must keep your workspace tidy and organized. When you lose focus, you essentially squander precious time. Take a couple of minutes daily to clean up your workspace. If your workspace is cluttered with old files, office stationery, or things you don't need, remove them. Your desk must be neat, organized, and tidy. Cleaning and decluttering can be relaxing.

Tip #9: Find Balance

To reduce the stress you feel, then it is unquestionably necessary that you balance your personal and professional life. You cannot concentrate only on one aspect of your life to get ahead. To avoid burnout in your daily life, learn to recognize the importance of work-life balance. The absence of this balance increases the stress you feel. Once you feel stressed, it becomes easier to indulge in bad habits, and these bad habits will eventually take away your concentration from your goals. While working, take a couple of breaks sometimes. You cannot concentrate on a specific task for over 45 minutes at a stretch. Once the 45 minutes are up, give yourself a break for five minutes. In this break, you can get yourself a cup of coffee, talk to someone you want, or maybe even just relax. Regardless of what you do, keep giving yourself a few mental breaks.

Tip #10: Get Rid of Distractions

It is not just decluttering that matters, but you must also remove distractions for improving your productivity. Decluttering your physical space is as important as decluttering the mental space available to you too. Our usual habits lean toward distractions and allow our minds to wander for longer than required. All these things merely lead to an additional waste of time. It could be in a colleague interrupting you while working, checking your social media, playing any games, or attending a call while in the meeting. All these things essentially take away your mental ability to concentrate on the task at hand. Also, don't try multitasking.

You might think you can do more things if you're working on various tasks simultaneously. Well, multitasking merely leads to wastage of your precious mental energy. Think of your entire attention span as a bucket. Every task you work on puts a small hole in this bucket. If you are working on several things at once, then multiple holes will form in this bucket, and it can hold no water within. So, get rid of distractions, concentrate on one thing at a task, and move onto the next only after completing the task at hand.

By following the simple tips discussed in this section, you can ensure that you are getting more things accomplished within the given time frame. If you follow these tips for a couple of weeks, you will notice a positive change in the way you spend your time.

Chapter Ten: Focus, Motivation, and Self-Discipline

Stay Focused and Motivated

What is the difference between those who succeed and everyone else? What do successful people do that most of us fail to do? Sure, talent, luck, and hard work matter. There is another critical aspect we all overlook, and it is the ability to keep going even when boredom strikes. We all talk about staying motivated and being passionate. People lose motivation or feel depressed when they believe successful people have unstoppable willpower and passion. They do have willpower and passion, but they also know how to keep going when boredom strikes. There is no magic pill they use to feel inspired and ready to tackle all the challenges. Those who succeed and wish to attain their goals don't allow their emotions to guide their actions. Top performers work through the border and embrace the daily practice and consistency required to attain them. It isn't easy to work when it isn't easy. Anyone can work when feeling pumped up and motivated. However, when this motivation falters, you must still keep going to attain your goals.

We live in a world filled with distractions from unlimited web access to constant messaging; staying focused and constructive can become difficult. In this section, you will learn about simple tips you can follow to stay motivated and focused on your goals.

Money Might Not Be Motivating

Money is important, and it can be a motivating factor. However, money cannot be the only motivating factor. Many people wrongly assume that money will motivate them to keep going. In the initial stages, it can work, but sustaining financial motivation becomes tricky if the work you are doing keeps dragging on. When you work long enough, you will realize money is not worth compromising on different aspects of your life. If the activities associated with your goal are tedious, tiring, or too complicated, then money cannot be a motivating factor. Also, if these activities are not in sync with who you are and what you want to do in life, setting and attaining goals will become tricky.

Are They Your Goals?

Another common obstacle in staying motivated and following through on goals is ensuring that the goals you have set are the ones you genuinely want to attain. At times, we set goals based on what others think or what others feel we should be doing. Instead of concentrating on what we want to do, we give undue importance to what others think. You can always ask others for their opinions but ensure that the goals you set hold some personal value for you. If they represent no personal values, you probably will prematurely give up on them. So, spend some time, follow the tips and steps discussed in the previous chapters to ensure your goals are your own. There is a significant difference between going after something that you want and what others want.

Visualizing the Results

A simple way to concentrate on your goals and keep up your motivation levels is by visualizing the result you wish to attain. Instead of getting bogged down by all the challenges or complexity of the goal, concentrate on how wonderful you will feel when you attain the goals. Visualize the result. How will you feel when you attain your goal? You'll probably feel relieved and incredibly excited. Concentrate on these two feelings to fuel you on days when you don't want to work. Attaining goals takes hard work, and this hard work can make you want to procrastinate. So, by reminding yourself of what you can achieve with your hard work, you can propel yourself toward attaining the desired results.

Breaking Down the Goals

When you look at a big goal, it can become quickly overwhelming. When it becomes overwhelming, you'll get scared about it, and the initial motivation associated with the goal will fade away. To avoid all this, it is better to break down the goals into simpler and manageable tasks. For instance, if your goal is to reorganize your closet, you can break it down into simpler tasks like reorganizing your shoes, winter clothing, bags, and so on. So, you will be a step closer to attaining your overall goal whenever you complete one simple task. Also, upon completion, you will feel a little satisfied with yourself and motivated to keep going.

Company Matters

The kind of company you maintain matters a lot when it comes to your overall attitude in life. If you surround yourself with people who give out positive energy, you will feel better about yourself. Engage in stimulating conversations about your passions with your close circle. If someone seems unsupportive of your goals, it is time to maintain some distance. Others need not agree with what you say, but you need no negative energy toward your goals. If naysayers surround you, you probably will quickly give up on the goals because you feel you do nothing. Instead, surround yourself with motivated, inspirational, and positive individuals. Their positivity will trickle into your life.

Start Organizing

Start decluttering your thoughts and organize them. Whenever you work on a big goal, a cluttered and overstimulated mind will sap you of all your energy. Instead of allowing yourself to get overwhelmed and drained out like this, it is better to declutter your mind. Sit down for a while and pay attention to all the different thoughts you have about your goals. You can note these thoughts in a journal, or you can talk to your loved ones about them. Once you have a list in place, dedicate a specific time for completing each task. It helps you get what you want without getting sidetracked or overwhelmed.

Concentrate On the Big Picture

Regardless of what you do, ensure that your main goal always stays in your mind. Even while dealing with unpleasant or menial tasks associated with the goal, don't lose sight of it. If you are running low on motivation, remind yourself that your goal is not just about completing a task but also about something much bigger than all this.

Letting Go

There are several factors in your life you cannot control. Instead of worrying about all the external factors you cannot control, it is better to concentrate on controlling and regulating factors. If you keep worrying about things you cannot do, you will feel paralyzed and stuck worrying about the future. Replace all the thoughts that start with "what if" to "I can." Don't contemplate the future. Since you cannot control it. However, you can certainly take action in the present to ensure that you create the kind of future you want.

Be Consistent

Ensure that you are consistent while working toward your goals. Every day make it a point to do at least one thing that puts you a step closer to your goal. It need not be anything significant. For instance, if weight loss is your goal, then make it a point you exercise for at least

30 minutes daily. On days you don't feel like exercising, make sure you are eating healthy and wholesome meals. If not, concentrate on something else you can do to stay on track and attain your goals. Unless you are consistent, your motivational levels are bound to falter.

Follow the simple tips discussed in this section to keep up your motivation levels while going after your life goals.

Developing Self-Discipline

To attain a goal, you need self-discipline. Self-discipline is the force that enables you to move forward and keep going even when you don't feel like doing it. You can keep performing, fulfilling your promises, and meeting all the deadlines essential for becoming successful. Without self-discipline, the momentum required to make progress will be absent. Self-discipline is your ability to regulate and work toward improvement. You can regulate your desires, feelings, and actions.

Self-discipline is about consistently taking small actions that gradually help develop good habits that propel you toward your goals. By integrating these habits into your daily life, it becomes easier to create a lifestyle in sync with your goals. It helps condition and rewires your mind to recognize the long-term rewards associated with every step you take while forgoing behaviors that might cause short-term pleasure. A disciplined mind not only sees but also realizes the importance of waking up early and getting a head start on the day instead of hitting the snooze button for some extra sleep.

Self-discipline is quintessential for becoming successful in all aspects of your life. All successful people are incredibly self-discipline. Self-discipline is the source of persistence, dedication, and inspiration required to overcome any obstacles and challenges that come along your way on the route to success. It enables you to realize and access your innate inner strength. It also improves your confidence and problem-solving abilities. Self-discipline helps you see the bigger picture and forces you to take action even when you don't want to.

Well, do you think you are self-disciplined? To be fair, this is one area in which most of us could use some extra help. The good news is that – as with any other habit – you can develop and improve your self-discipline. In this section, let us look at some simple steps you can follow to develop self-discipline.

Step #1: Understand Your Goals

The first step is to envision and define your goals – what they mean to you and how you want to achieve them. There are two questions you must ask yourself to do this.

• What does success mean to you regarding your goal?

• What are the different steps you must take to reach your destination?

Unless you have some clarity about your goals, you cannot develop self-discipline.

Step #2: Personal Values

What are your personal values? What does your goal mean to you? What is the driving force that keeps you going? What is the value you can attain by achieving a goal? You can develop self-discipline once you start creating personal value in all the goals you set. Unless these goals are valuable to you, you will not want to achieve them, or procrastination will creep in. To avoid all this, you must find your inspirations and motivations and continuously remind yourself of the same.

Step #3: Finding a Role Model

Whatever goal you have, you will not be the only person with that goal. Therefore, spend some time trying to look at all the people who accomplished the same goal you are trying to. For instance, if weight loss is your goal, you can look for inspiration by talking to a friend who achieved the same goal as you. By talking to such people, you can come up with a list of specific behaviors that might have empowered them and given them the strength to keep going even in the face of adversities. You can also learn of the different mistakes they made along the way and try avoiding them. Besides this, you will also learn about all the possible challenges you might face while working toward attaining your goals.

Step #4: What Are The Challenges?

Working toward a goal is seldom easy. So, be prepared to run into particular challenges and obstacles along the way. It would be foolish to expect smooth sailing throughout the journey. All the obstacles you face will challenge your resolve and might even make you question yourself. Once you know the different challenges you might face, you can avoid or overcome them. For instance, if weight loss is your goal, then one obstacle you might face is dealing with the urge to binge on unhealthy foods. So, what can you do? You can come up with healthier alternatives to your favorite snacks or maybe devise an alternate plan to overcome the temptation.

Step #5: Changes

You don't have to change your entire personality to attain a goal. However, there are certain habits or behaviors you can develop to increase your chances of success. Think about your goal, and then make a list of different qualities and skills you need to attain that goal. To do this, you can once again look at successful people and their stories and list their traits and characteristics. Compare yourself with such people, and you will realize the different habits you must develop.

Step #6: Environment Matters

Unless your environment is conducive to growth, you will struggle with self-discipline even if you are in the right state of mind. Your usual environment must support your goals and the habits you must form to attain those goals. For instance, you cannot stay focused on a specific task if you work in a noisy environment. So, you must work on creating an environment that supports your goals and growth.

Step #7: Make a Commitment

Consider all the factors mentioned up until now. Now, it is time to create a detailed plan of action that enables you to make progress. What are the different actions you can take daily? How will you deal with obstacles? What are the changes you must make? Prioritize all the tasks, create milestones, and set certain rewards that enable you to move toward your goals.

Step #8: Tracking Your Progress

A simple way to stay focused, motivated, and disciplined is by turning your progress. Maintain a journal that enables you to see the progress you make and areas where there is scope for improvement. Note all things working for you and that make you feel good. Also, don't forget to include details about things that don't work for you. Periodically look at the journal entries, make adjustments as required, and it will help you stay focused.

Step #9: Understand Your Emotions

Most of us allow our emotions to regulate us instead of regulating our emotions. Therefore, learn to identify and interpret your emotions so you can effectively deal with various situations in life. If things don't feel as they are supposed to, or like you're expected, explore other approaches. Don't allow your emotions to guide your decisions.

Step #10: Inspiration

Maintaining self-discipline becomes a little complicated when dealing with adversity. It is where inspiration steps into the picture. You can explore different sources of inspiration like mindfulness, meditation, reading books, talking to your mentors, watching inspirational movies, and so on. It is easy to keep going when you feel inspired.

Follow these ten simple steps to develop self-discipline. Don't expect any miraculous changes overnight. It takes some time and effort to form a new habit. So, be patient and commit yourself.

Chapter Eleven: Goal Reviewing and Reflection

Benefits of Goal Reviewing and Reflection

Your work doesn't end once you set goals. You need to continuously and consistently work toward attaining those goals. Along the way, you must also review and reflect upon all these goals and the progress you make. Regardless of the goal you set, by reviewing your goals consistently, you can produce consistent results. When you lose sight of your goals, it might make you feel like you are fighting an uphill battle, and it can harm your inclination to keep going. So, let us look at the different benefits of reviewing and reflecting on the goals you set.

An essential benefit of establishing a goal is that it enables you to determine the course of action you must take to reach your desired destination. By reviewing your plan of action or the quintessential roadmap daily, you'll be better equipped to execute any plan you come up with. When you keep reminding yourself of the different steps you must take, it will come to you automatically. Then, reaching your target or goal becomes an inevitable destination. Without all this, you merely end up with a destination with no roadmap of reaching it.

Your goals will be forgotten if you don't keep repeating them. You might have probably listened to a song that got stuck in your mind, and you kept replaying it in your mind later. However, this memory will only last for a couple of days. If you stop listening to the song, you will quickly forget the lyrics. Likewise, you must frequently review your goals to ensure that you can recall the steps you must take to attain them. Besides that, it also enables you to understand the different benchmarks for reviewing the goals. The more you do this, the probability of implementing the desired actions increases. When you frequently review the steps, it eventually creates a new neural pathway in your mind to not forget about your goals. When your goals stay in your memory, every action you take consciously or unconsciously goes back to the goal you want to achieve.

When you review your goals, it adds to the daily motivation you feel. Make it a point to review your goals when you wake up and once before you go to sleep. In the morning, remind yourself of your purpose and all that you wish to accomplish. Before you go to sleep, reflect on the day you had and all the highlights. If you feel there is some scope for improvement, don't forget to make the required changes. For instance, if you realized that you spent more time answering emails than you were supposed to, you can think about automating certain emails' responses.

If you don't review your goals, you will eventually lose the desire to attain them. When you lose this vital desire, the goal loses its value along the way. If there is no sense of urgency, desire often loses its value. Goals will also eventually lose value when you don't review them. Ensure that you review your goals once every day to avoid any mindless action. When you keep thinking about your goals, your thoughts become actions. Once you take action, you can attain your goals.

You cannot achieve a goal overnight, and it takes consistent hard work and effort. So, whenever you make some progress, don't forget to review it. When you see that you are making progress, it not only makes you feel happy, but it gives you a sense of accomplishment that enables you to work toward your goals. When your personal value increases, your self-worth increases. Even if the progress isn't significant, the knowledge you made some progress will keep you going.

Steps to Follow

Now that you're aware of the different benefits review and reflection offers, it is time to incorporate certain simple practices into your daily routine. Here are a couple of different tips you can follow.

Relevancy of the Goal

Every goal you establish is based on your existing situation in life. Since life doesn't exist in a vacuum, change is inevitable. When your life changes, you must review your goals to ensure they are still relevant. For instance, if your goal was to get a promotion, but you changed jobs before accomplishing the goal, it is time to review and tweak the goal to meet your new requirements. If the goal loses its relevance, then you will have no desire to achieve it. So, ask yourself whether your situation has changed significantly? If there have been any significant changes, is the goal still relevant? Are you still keen on attaining your goals? Is this what you want to do? Remember, unless the goal is irrelevant, you will not have the motivation to attain them. Remind yourself why you set the goal in the first place, and introspect whether the reasons hold true for you in the present scenario.

Measuring Your Progress

Regardless of the goal you set, you must be able to track and measure the progress. You can use a ranking system or even an actual measure like weight to measure any progress you make. For instance, if your goal is to lose 20 pounds within six months, then a simple measure you can use is your bodyweight. If you notice any changes in your body weight in a positive direction, it means you are successfully working toward your goals. Likewise, if you notice you are gaining weight, it means you might need to change your diet or exercise routine to get back on track. To measure any progress you make, go back to your starting point and compare it with your situation. If you notice an upward swing, it means you are closer to attaining your goals than you were earlier. If you think you're not on track, it is time for a little self-introspection. It is where reflection comes into the picture. Reflect upon all that you did and the reasons you went off track. With a little self-reflection, you can quickly identify the different obstacles that pushed you off course. By taking corrective action to overcome these obstacles, you can quickly get back on track.

Action Plan

Your goal is the end destination, whereas your action plan is the roadmap you can use to reach the destination. If you don't use this plan, then how can you ever reach your destination? Take some time and think about your plan of action and any other alternate options available. Don't worry if you need to make specific changes to your goals. Change is an inevitable part of life, and you cannot shy away from it. Therefore, adapt yourself to the change, and try to reframe your goals to stay relevant and suit your needs.

If you set any deadline for yourself, it is time to review whether you have met those deadlines. If you fail to meet deadlines, there is a reason for it. Deadlines are established since it helps build momentum. Maybe the deadlines were unrealistic, or perhaps other urgent activities needed your immediate attention. Reflect upon why you missed the deadlines. If your deadlines were impractical, then come up with something more practical. Regardless of your plan of action, ensure that you allow a little wiggle room for yourself. Life is unpredictable, and things can change in the blink of an eye. Therefore, try to make some room to accommodate all these unpredictable changes.

If you think your timeframe and the action plan are both ideal, then stick to it. However, in your review, if you notice you couldn't, then understand the reasons for the same.

Resources

Do you have sufficient resources to support your goals? It could be in the form of time, support, information, or even finances. Is anything preventing you from attaining your goals? Do you think you are honestly struggling to attain the goal? Regardless of what it is, never spread yourself out too thin. If you do this, you will eventually burn yourself out and increase the stress you experience. To prevent all this, you might need to readjust your plan of action. Maybe you need a while longer than you thought. If that's the case, then it is okay to alter your deadlines. However, ensure that the deadlines are realistic and don't place your goals on the backburner for too long. If you do this, any momentum you gained until this point will soon dispel. If you are running short of resources, then maybe it is time to consider how you can increase your resources.

Review

How did you prepare and plan for a specific goal you want to attain? While reviewing, was there anything in the review that set your alarm bells off? Do you think you're still on track to attaining your goals? Do you still have sight of the big picture? Is there something holding you back? Are there any bad habits or weaknesses preventing you from attaining your goals? Can you draw on any of your strengths to help yourself? Carefully consider all these questions while you review the progress you make. Here are a couple of other questions you can ask yourself during the review and reflection session.

• What are the different things you are doing that are enabling you to work toward your goal? (Well, keep doing these things and keep up your excellent work!)

- Are you happy with the progress you are making? (If yes, then you are on the right track. If not, you must make changes to your plan of action to increase your progress.)

- Is the goal more manageable than you thought it would be?

- Is the goal harder than you initially believed? (If yes, then you need to work on improving your motivation levels to attain the goal. you can use a vision board.)

- Do you think you need to take small steps?

- Do you think you need to take more significant steps, and will you be able to do this?

- How can you improve yourself to attain your goals?

- Are you excited about the goal? Do you like working on your goal? (If yes, then it means you chose the right goal. if not, it is time to review your goal and perhaps replace it with something you enjoy.)

- Are you sticking to your core values while you work toward your goals? (Go back and review your core values. If you are diverting from them, then maybe you need to replace your goal. If you compromise on your core values, it can cause unnecessary internal conflict, preventing you from working on your goals.)

Reflection (Success/Failure Analysis)

Once you work toward your goals, you will find a couple of victories, and for some failures. Success and failure are two sides of the same coin. One cannot exist without the other. So, you must maintain a positive attitude, regardless of the outcome. Never give up on your goal because you might encounter an obstacle or experience failure. True failure is when you stop working on your goal and believe it is the end of the road. It is all about your mindset. Whenever you feel, don't give up. Instead, use this precious opportunity to analyze all the things that went wrong. It enables you to gather knowledge that will improve any goal-setting process you undertake.

Concentrate on the failures, but don't forget about all the victories that come your way. Don't get so overwhelmed thinking or worrying about failure that you forget to celebrate your success. Analyze all the events that led to your success. It will enable you to realize the things that contribute to the achievement of your goals. Once you realize these things, you can spend more of your time and energy engaging in such practices that are desirable. It enables you to understand what works for you. You must keep reviewing your goals as you work toward attaining them. It's not just review, but you must also reflect on the outcomes.

This review identifies all the things you did well and the ones you didn't. Most important, it enables you to understand how you can improve or the things you can do differently in the future to meet your goals.

Check-Ins

A short-term goal is something that you wish to attain within a month. For such goals, you must review them at least once every week. You don't have to review it daily, but try to do it on every alternate day. A quarterly goal is a goal you wish to accomplish within three months. Ensure that you review it every week to ensure you are on the right track. A semi-annual goal is something you want to achieve within six months. You must review it at least once a month. If you think it is essential, you can review it once a week. An annual goal is something you wish to accomplish within a year. You must review it twice every year and can include it in your quarterly review. If you have any long-term goals (five years or longer), don't forget to review them twice every year.

While reviewing these goals, ensure that you don't lose focus on the smaller goals you set. Every goal is equally important. If you get overwhelmed by setting multiple goals, then stick to one or, at the most, five goals and work on them consistently.

If you are maintaining a journal or an app to check your progress, ensure there is a sufficient place to add notes as time goes by. You might need to slightly modify individual goals or make notes when you cannot achieve a specific goal. Regardless of the outcome, don't give up on the goal and keep up your hard work.

Chapter Twelve: Obstacles and Mistakes in Goal Setting

Common Obstacles to Goal Setting

There are a couple of common obstacles you must avoid while setting goals. These obstacles can make all the difference between success and failure for attaining your goals. So, let us look at them and how to avoid them in this section.

Too Many Commitments

We all have plenty of things we have to accomplish daily. It is not just your daily chores, but you must also concentrate on the goals you want to attain. So, how can you squeeze in more things while concentrating on your goals? The simplest way to make the most of the time available to you while concentrating on your set goals is by eliminating, automating, and delegating certain tasks. All the things you considered neither essential nor urgent must be eliminated from your daily agenda. Try automating your daily chores. You can automate your bill payments and email responses. Every minute you save is an additional minute to concentrate on your goals. If you know someone else can do the same task efficiently, then delegate. When you delegate, you can concentrate only on the things that matter and require your attention.

Stressing Out

Stop stressing out. You cannot accomplish your goals if you keep stressing out about them. External factors can cause stress, but eventually, it all boils down to how you deal with it. The workload does not stress you out; it is the way you carry it. That adds to the stress. So, it is time to work on reducing and regulating your stress levels. Stress is not just tiring mentally, but it can also harm your physical wellbeing. You can try meditation, take regular breaks while working, and add some exercise to your daily routine. You don't have to exercise or meditate for hours on end. Set about 20 to 30 minutes aside daily for de-stressing. Once your mind is free from stress, it becomes easier to concentrate on your goals. Also, it gives you the mental energy required to review and reflect on the goals you have set for yourself.

Time Constraints

Time is an essential and limited resource. You can feel rather frustrated when you have too many things to accomplish within a short period. We all have a fixed number of hours available at our disposal. So, making the most of it is quintessential for attaining a goal. Ensure that you have a good morning routine. Wake up early in the morning and concentrate on the most critical tasks of the day. When you get these important tasks out of the way, it becomes easier to allocate the available time toward all the other tasks. Also, make it a point not to stay up late at night. Use the different tips about time management in the previous section to develop a daily schedule for yourself.

Ensure that you get at least 6 to 7 hours of good quality and undisturbed sleep every night. Your body and mind need sufficient rest if you want them to keep performing optimally. Remember the age-old saying, "The early bird catches the worm?" It will do you good to remember this when it comes to time management.

Don't Try to be a Perfectionist

We all desire perfection, but if you get obsessed with perfection, you will get nothing done. No plan will ever be perfect, and you will keep second-guessing every decision you make until it reaches your desired level of perfection. To attain your goals, ensure that you are *taking action* instead of just planning out every detail. At times, the best course of action is to take the first step instead of thinking about it. Use the 80% approach to lose the perfectionist attitude and overcome procrastination. It essentially says that you must invent, execute, or take some action, but not do it to its fullest. You will only complete about 80% of the task. This increases your confidence and builds momentum. The 80% must include the trickiest tasks you must undertake to attain your goal. When this significant chunk is out of the way, you will be left with 20% of the easy work. You might even delegate the rest to someone else.

Lack of Energy

Sometimes, you think, "I have no energy to do anything else." After a tiring day, you might not want to work on your goals. There will be days when life can easily overwhelm you or get in the way. You must plan your days wisely and use your energy optimally. Your overall energy is like a freshly baked pie. Whenever you add an activity to your daily routine, one slice of this pie is removed. So, carefully consider whether the tasks you partake in daily add value to your life or not.

So, ensure that you take good care of yourself. Self-care is your responsibility, and there is no way in which you can delegate it to others. You cannot do away with self-care. Unless you care for your body, mind, and soul, they will not serve you optimally. It is not just about planning your days, but you must be considerate of your energy at your disposal if you try to do too many things at once, the potential of a burnout increases. When this happens, any motivation you had toward attaining the goal will quickly fade away.

Losing Your Drive

Losing your motivation or the desire to keep going is one obstacle you must never overlook. During the initial stage, you might hit the ground running, make some good progress, and then suddenly, you no longer have the drive to keep going. The road to success is never straightforward, and it keeps meandering in unexpected ways. Whenever your motivation tank is running dangerously low, it is time to remind yourself of the reasons you want to attain your goal. You must thoroughly understand your goal and your reasons for wanting to achieve that goal. Unless you understand all this, you will eventually lose the motivation to keep going. You can use the different tips about motivation in the previous chapters to ensure that you don't lose your drive.

Goal-Setting Mistakes to Avoid

Goals can inspire and motivate you to become successful. They give you a clear sense of direction and enable you to effectively prioritize the different tasks you must complete. When you make certain mistakes while setting goals, these goals become a burden and will hinder you instead of inspiring you. Setting goals might seem like a piece of cake. However, unless you do it right, your chances of success are low. Unless you set practical goals, you cannot make the right decisions. Unless you make the right decisions, your overall productivity will suffer. Poor decisions are directly proportional to poor results. So, to turn your life around, then you must set practical goals for yourself.

Mistakes are life's way of teaching you important lessons. However, it doesn't mean you must keep making mistakes to learn. You can learn a lot from the mistakes that others make. In this section, let us look at some common goal-setting mistakes and how you can avoid them.

Tasks vs. Goals

A common mistake many people make while setting goals is that they set tasks instead of goals. A practical goal helps challenge you and unlock your potential. The goals must be challenging so you can grow as a person while working on attaining them. If the goal you set can be achieved with no growth, then you have not established a goal for yourself. Instead, you merely set up a couple of tasks you must complete.

Internal Conflict

It has been mentioned time and again in this book: the goal you set must never directly conflict with your identity or purpose. The goals must be consistent with the kind of person you are, want to be, and your values. Unless they serve you, you cannot work on attaining them. For instance, if honesty is one of your core values, then the goals you set must not encourage dishonest behavior. If there is any conflict of interest, it causes severe internal dilemmas that can demotivate you instead of inspiring you.

For Others

Ensure that the goal you set is only for yourself and not for others. Well, if your goals are based on any expectations that others will change, you are setting yourself up for disappointment. Set goals only for yourself. You cannot control the way others are, regardless of how hard you wish it otherwise. The only thing you can control is your life and your reactions. If you set goals for others, you have no control over the goals. Also, you have no right to determine how the other person is supposed to live their lives. You can state your opinions and preferences, but you cannot dictate terms about how others must live. For instance, your goal might be to lead a healthier life. To do this, you might have stopped drinking alcohol. Merely because you did this, it doesn't mean others have to follow. You can encourage them to do this, but you cannot force them.

Out of Your Control

You cannot set goals for things beyond your purview of control. The only thing you can control is your thoughts and actions. These are the two things you can always control. If your goals depend on others or on things you cannot control, you are setting yourself up for failure and disappointment. For instance, a goal like "I will get promoted if my boss changes," is not something you can control.

Too Generic

Your goals cannot inspire or motivate you if they aren't detailed. If your goals are vague and generic, your desire to follow suit will reduce. A generic goal might be to lead a happy life, become healthy and fit, or earn more money. These goals explain a generic state of being and not the specific steps you must take to attain them. If you aren't aware of the steps you must take, you can never reach your destination. Therefore, the goals must be detail-oriented. For instance, "I want to lose weight" is a generic goal. An explicit goal is, "I want to lose 20 pounds within six months." When the goal is detailed, it becomes easier to flesh out a plan of action for attaining it.

What You Don't Want

We all know the things we don't like or don't desire. For instance, you might not want to be unhappy, unhealthy, and so on. These are not goals; they are personal statements about your dislikes. Your goal must concentrate on the things you want and desire in life. They should be related to your vision, mission, and core values. Unless a goal is in sync with all this, it cannot be attained. You must know the action you must take to attain the goals. So, start concentering on the positive aspects of a goal instead of concentrating on the things you don't desire.

Looking for Perfection

If you desire perfection in everything you do, you are setting yourself up for disappointment. Remember that you are a human, and you are bound to make a couple of poor decisions and mistakes. If you have a perfectionist attitude in mind, these mistakes will seem like a failure. If you desire absolute perfection from your goal, you are setting yourself up for unnecessary disappointment and failure. Instead, ensure that you are realistic about your goals. Regardless of the time taken, the goal you set must be realistic. It doesn't mean you must not dream big. You can, but ensure that you can also attain them through hard work.

Setting mistakes while establishing goals can seriously harm any progress you make. At times, it can also be the source of incredible stress while you push yourself to achieve goals in direct conflict with your beliefs or values. Goal setting is powerful and will motivate you, provided you do it properly. Go through the different mistakes in this section and tips to avoid them while setting new goals.

Chapter Thirteen: Goal Achieved – Now What?

Take a moment and rejoice in your victory. You have attained your goal! It has been quite a journey, and you have successfully reached your destination. So, what can you do now that you have attained your goals? After you pat yourself on the back for making it this far, it is time to keep practicing good habits daily. All the changes you made to your life and mindset while working toward your goals must stay with you. You cannot forget about them or stop practicing them after you attain your goal. Goal setting is a lifelong process. You can take a break in the middle, but you can never stop if you want to be successful. All the different tips you learned about setting goals, focus, motivation, and productivity must be implemented every day. Becoming self-disciplined is a valuable trait you must never let go of. So, what now? It is time to keep up your motivation levels while developing certain desirable habits that will enable you to stay successful in life.

In this section, you'll learn about simple steps you can follow to develop daily habits for maintaining your overall sense of motivation and self-discipline.

Developing Daily Habits

Decide

You cannot develop a good habit unless you make a conscious decision to do so. To be more self-discipline, it must be a conscious decision. So, it is time to decide what you want to start or stop doing. If you're used to procrastination, then a good habit is to avoid procrastination and instill self-discipline. You must be sure of the way and time at which you wish to incorporate the new behavior. For instance, if your goal is to wake up early every day to concentrate on your goals, you must fix a specific time for that exercise. You cannot just state, "I want to wake up early," instead, it must be something like, "I want to wake up at 6:30 am daily." So, whenever the alarm goes off in the morning, you will know it is time to get out of bed and work on your goals. While deciding this, ensure that the timing is something that you can work with consistently. For instance, if you know that you will be pulling a couple of all-nighters in the next ten days, then waking up at 6:30 A.M. is not realistic.

To incorporate a habit, ensure that it is something you can do daily regardless of the circumstances. If you are confident that it isn't something you'll do consistently, you are merely setting yourself up for disappointment.

Talk to Others

If you are trying to develop a new habit, then talk to your loved ones about the same. Explain the different reasons you want to develop a new habit. It enables you to become more determined and disciplined while you go about learning the new habit. When you know that others expect something specific from you, it puts a little pressure and creates added responsibility. When you know you are accountable to others, your motivation to follow through on your promise also increases. So, discuss your goals with your loved ones. There will be days when you run a little low on motivation. In such instances, your support system can step in and give you the motivation they require to keep going.

No Exceptions

To develop a new habit, there are no exceptions to this rule. Stick to the habit of the routine you wish to inculcate, especially during the formative stages. Now is the time to be a little hard on yourself and don't allow yourself off the hook easily. You are responsible for yourself, and you are accountable for the same. If you wish to develop a new habit, then accountability is quintessential, and no one else can do it for you. Keep a check on yourself, and don't give in to any orders that will deviate you from the new habit you wish to incorporate. You can quickly come up with excuses for rationalizing something you were not supposed to do. For instance, if your goal is to wake up at 6:30 am daily, you must wake up at 6:30 am with no excuses. The only reason you're trying to incorporate a new habit is your improvement. So, it means making a little extra effort during the initial stages. Once you get the hang of it, you will realize that your efforts were truly worth it.

Visualization

A great way to develop a new habit is by visualizing the habit. Think about how wonderful you will feel when you behave in a specific manner. The more time you spend visualizing yourself acting as if you have acquired the habit, the easier it will be to incorporate the same. While visualizing, ensure that your visualization is detailed. For instance, if the new habit you wish to develop is to be more confident, then visualize how wonderful you would feel when you are as confident as you want. Also, by doing this, you are automatically prompting your mind to enable you to act and behave more confidently. Visualization and self-programming go hand-in-hand.

Positive Affirmations

We all tend to have a continuous internal dialogue with ourselves. We think different thoughts, critique our behavior, we praise our effort, and so on. All this is known as your internal talk or self-talk. When this self-talk is predominantly negative, you cannot feel better about yourself. So, pay attention to your self-talk. Ensure that your conversations with yourself are more optimistic. You need to pay a little conscious attention to prevent negative thoughts from creeping up. Even if negative thoughts come up, don't give them too much importance. It doesn't mean you must prevent yourself from thinking negative thoughts; it merely means you must learn to replace them with something more positive. A simple way to do this is by using positive affirmations.

Positive affirmations are statements you can keep repeating to rewire your subconscious. For instance, if your inner critic keeps saying, "I cannot do this," then you must replace it with something more positive. Like, "I cannot do this right now, but I will eventually get there." If you are trying to be more confident, then squish all negative thoughts, replace them with something more positive, like "I am confident." By repeating these positive affirmations daily, you instill a sense of positivity into your subconscious. This positivity is bound to reflect in different aspects of your life. Remember that for positive affirmations to work, you must practice them consistently. Make it a daily habit of setting aside 5 to 10 minutes in the morning to indulge in some positive affirmations.

Rewards

An essential aspect of incorporating a new habit is to create a reward system. Whenever you do something desirable, don't forget to reward yourself for it. By creating a positive association between your actions, and the reward, your motivation to keep at it will increase. You need no one else to cheer or motivate you. Motivation comes from within. So, don't forget to treat yourself whenever you do something desirable. If a daily habit you wish to incorporate is to be more confident and assertive, congratulate yourself whenever you say no! It could be something as simple as watching an episode of your favorite series or maybe even buying some nail polish. The rewards can be simple and need not be anything extravagant.

Persistence

To develop a new habit, you must be persistent and consistent in your first. If you stick by a promise for a week and then give up, it makes little sense. It would be a waste of your time and effort. You must keep practicing the behavior until it comes to you automatically. Once this happens, you no longer have to make any conscious effort to do or not do something. You will feel uncomfortable whenever you deviate from the habit you worked hard to form. Remember that your brain needs consistency in developing new habits. So, learn to be persistent and don't give up.

Make the Habits Stick

It is not just about developing a habit, but you must ensure that the habit you develop *sticks.* If you follow a habit for a couple of weeks and then forget about it, it is counterintuitive to the entire purpose of learning a habit. In this section, let us look at specific simple tips to ensure that any habit you've developed sticks.

To make a habit stick, you must be consistent. If you aim to exercise regularly, ensure that you exercise every day for at least one month. If you exercise once or twice a week, it will become difficult to form a new habit. Consistency is quintessential for developing a new habit. You cannot form a habit if you do things occasionally and not consistently.

To make a habit stick, commit yourself to it for at least 30 days. Bring out your calendar; count the days until the time is up. After the first 30 days, the habit will come to you naturally with no conscious decisions.

Always start simple. If you attempt to do everything at once, you get nothing done. You cannot make a massive overhaul in one day. You cannot change your life in a day. Therefore, learn to be patient with yourself. If you aim to read more daily, then instead of trying to read an entire book on a day, you can start by reading 20 pages daily. After a while, you'll get the hang of it, and you can read for longer. If the habit you try to incorporate clashes with your usual schedule, then the chances of incorporating it into your daily routine decrease.

It would help if you created a trigger to remind yourself of the habit you wish to develop. This trigger can be a ritual or a cue you can follow before executing a habit. For instance, if your idea is to exercise regularly, then a trigger could be drinking a protein shake in the evening before exercising. Whenever you are drinking the protein shake, it is a silent reminder to your mind about the habit you want to develop.

Stop expecting perfection from yourself. It is okay to strive for perfection, but expecting perfection all the time is a recipe for disaster. You can be a little hard on yourself, especially when you don't stick to your habit during an initial couple of days. However, don't be critical to the extent that it dominates any motivation you have. Be patient and compassionate toward yourself. What might work for others doesn't necessarily have to work for you. So, a routine that seems to have worked for a friend might not work for you. If that's the case, don't be disappointed, and merely think of different ways to attain your goals.

Tips for Daily Motivation

Learning to motivate yourself is an important life skill. Motivation isn't random – even if it feels like it is at times. Once you understand how motivation works, it becomes easier to stop procrastination and overcome any inner resistance toward working on your goals. Also, motivation makes your life easier and enjoyable. Since you no longer have to force yourself to do something but experience an inherent desire to do it, life gets easier. For instance, when you feel like doing something, the chances of getting things done high. Likewise, when you don't feel like doing something, you need the motivation to keep going.

Many people wrongly believed that motivation doesn't last. Well, do you brush your teeth daily? Why do you do this? You do it to keep your teeth healthy and clean. Likewise, learning to motivate yourself is not a one-time thing. It is something you must work on daily. Unless you commit yourself to it, you cannot stay motivated. In this section, let's look at simple habits you can follow in your daily life to stay motivated about your goals.

Take a Cold Shower

Whenever you feel demotivated, wash your face with some cold water. If you are at home, take a long, cold shower. A cold shower can quickly jolt you awake and clear your mind. It also helps improve your overall energy levels. As soon as the cold water hits your skin, your body's natural stress response is triggered. During this period, stay calm for 10 to 15 seconds, control your breathing, and try to silence your mind. After these 15 seconds, you will notice that the shower isn't as bad as you thought it initially would be. You will feel awake and energized even if you stay under a cold shower for a minute.

Review Your Goals

Don't forget to review your goals daily. No, it differs from obsessing about them. It merely means you must consciously analyze all the tasks you accomplished on any given day. While doing this, assume a neutral perspective and don't be judgmental. If you notice there is scope for improvement, then you can always work on it.

Start Reading

Reading the stories of successful people can motivate you. Spend some time and read self-development or business books. Learn to feed your mind with positive messages, and you will feel more empowered. You can also stumble upon invaluable lessons from reading such books. By reading, you are consciously shifting your mind to focus on a growth mindset. Reading is also a great way to relax after a stressful day. If you are not keen on reading, then there's no time like the present to develop this habit. Even reading for about 15 minutes in the morning can motivate you. If not, reading, maybe you can watch some inspirational videos.

Your Environment Matters

Regardless of what you want to believe, the environment you spend your time and influences your motivation levels. Your environment influences the way you think, feel, and behave. Your environment consists of the company you keep and the direct environment like your workplace or home. Your environment can either support your goals or prevent you from accomplishing anything in life. For instance, if those around you are distracting you from working, then you cannot get anything done at work. Eventually, you will lose all interest and motivation to keep working.

- Who are the people who support and inspire you?
- Are you around people who hold you back?
- Who are the ones that make me feel better?
- Who are the ones that make you feel worse?
- Do you learn anything from the people you spend time with?
- Does your usual circle drain you out of your energy?

Your answers to these questions will help you understand whether you are spending your time in a good company or not. If you are around toxic people who hold you back, then you cannot become successful. So, pay attention to the company you keep. If your gut tells you something is off, it will do you good to listen to that inner voice!

Conclusion

If you are tired of living your life with no purpose or feel like you're wasting your precious resources, then it is time to set some goals for yourself. You can set professional, personal, health, fitness, lifestyle, or any other goals you want to. The sky is the limit when it comes to setting goals. However, ensure that the goals you set are in sync with your values and vision in life. The different tips and steps you can follow to do this have been discussed in this book in great detail. This book is the ideal guide anyone could use to turn their life around.

In this book, you were given all the information you require to set goals and develop plans and actions to attain those goals. You no longer have to depend on willpower or motivation to attain your goals. Long gone are the days when people believed these two factors were quintessential for attaining goals. By following the simple, actionable tips and steps in this book, you can attain the success you have always desired.

Using the different lazy goal setting hacks in this book and the tips to understand your reasons for setting a specific goal, you can improve your chances of success. Use vision boards and mind mapping for improving your clarity of the goals you have set. Follow the different tips to improve focus, motivation, and self-discipline in this book, and you will see a positive change in your overall life, not just your life but even your attitude toward life. You no longer have to sit by and watch life as it passes you by. Using the actionable tips and steps in this book, you can assume a proactive approach to life instead of a passive one. However, your job doesn't end after you attain your goal. Setting and attaining goals is a lifelong journey. So, keep at it until you have carved out the future you always wished for. Unlock the secrets to setting goals by using the information in this book.

Remember that the key to your successful life lies in your hands. You have the power to turn your life around for the better. You can have the kind of life you want to. The only obstacle you must overcome is your mindset. So, what are you waiting for? All that is left for you to do is to get started *right away.*

www.ingramcontent.com/pod-product-compliance
Lightning Source LLC
Chambersburg PA
CBHW071903090426
42811CB00004B/730

https://www.bolde.com/lazy-girls-guide-setting-goals/

https://www.youtube.com/watch?v=RlGQsAX7q8w,

https://www.mindmeister.com/blog/mind-mapping-benefits-who-needs-mind-maps/

https://productivityland.com/best-mind-mapping-software/

https://blog.mindvalley.com/vision-board/

https://www.tinypulse.com/blog/10-ways-to-meet-your-goals-with-time-management

https://www.entrepreneur.com/article/299336

https://www.holstee.com/blogs/mindful-matter/three-ways-reflection-can-influence-your-goals

https://www.pickthebrain.com/blog/top-5-reasons-reviewing-goals-must-success/

https://www.sparringmind.com/good-habits/

https://medium.com/personal-growth-lab/6-daily-habits-to-make-motivation-flow-effortlessly-c4156661e221

http://www.motivade.com/blog/2013/08/how-to-stay-motivated-daily/

References

https://www.achieve-goal-setting-success.com/personality.html,

https://www.lifereaction.com/great-goal-setting-personality-type/

https://www.youtube.com/watch?v=54aFTZ9POw4,

https://www.tlnt.com/6-reasons-not-to-use-smart-goals-for-everything/

https://www.employeeconnect.com/blog/difference-between-core-values-mission-vision-statements-and-goals/

https://www.greycampus.com/blog/project-management/personal-vision-mission-statement-how-do-you-build-them

https://www.youtube.com/watch?v=Lp_GOrM16Xc

https://www.youtube.com/watch?v=mBLGngFI5Ec

https://www.youtube.com/watch?v=BzAaOgzjPik,

https://www.youtube.com/watch?v=GOfl2sbgPhk

https://www.youtube.com/watch?v=WEaHtroHuoU

https://www.youtube.com/watch?v=EBgugeKaJa8

https://www.thelazygeniuscollective.com/blog/goals

https://medium.com/accelerated-intelligence/if-you-want-to-be-massively-successful-do-not-set-ambitious-goals-according-to-studies-affa9cd39f5d

Here's another book by Deon Hillman that you might like